REVIEWS OF U
MASQUERADE

"This book is truly a revelation. I cannot say enough about how compelling I found it to be... Superb."

Joseph Lamm, Recording Artist, Poet

"Before reading this book, grab your highlighter. You will find so many pieces of great information that you will want to remember, your book will probably glow in the dark like mine."

Don Bursell, Entertainer

"'Unmasking' has really opened my eyes... I had been more influenced by movies, books, TV... than the Bible, facts, and research!"

Tom Worcester, Aerospace Engineer

"... a valuable resource to any who might be curious about the crossover between illusion and their faith ... "

Dr. James Phipps, Professor

"Well researched and I will be reading again... this book will make a great gift for friends and family. I give it 5 stars!"

Mardi Cameron, Avid Reader

"Five Stars!! Once you start, you won't want to put it down... I can't believe how much power I've been giving Satan!"

Jennifer Kuhlman, Sales Account Manager

"5 stars—I read this book to learn what is behind the smoke and mirrors of magic and illusions, and came away with an even deeper belief in what is real- my faith in God. Bravo to the authors!"

Harriet Keith, Journalist, Business Consultant

"Loved it—5 stars! These authors deliver what we need to know about dealing with deception, demonology, and other matters of life and death."

Kim Newhouse, Home School Mom

"... filled with good stories. 'Unmasking the Masquerade' will make you think about what you believe about the paranormal and why... ."

Brian Frank, Minister of Education

UNMASKING THE MASQUERADE

II Timothy 1:7

Unmasking the Masquerade

Three Illusionists Investigate Deception, Fear, and the Supernatural

Rod Robison

Dr. Toby A. Travis and Adrian Van Vactor

Foreword by

André Kole

Printed in the United States of America

Library of Congress Control Number: 2016963537

Cataloguing data:

Robison, Rod, Toby A. Travis, Ed.D., Adrian Van Vactor
Unmasking the Masquerade: Three Illusionists Investigate Deception, Fear, and the Supernatural

ISBN 978-09962067-9-2 (paperback ed.)

ISBN 978-09962067-7-8 (hardback ed.)

1. Persuasion (Psychology) 2. Fear of spirits 3. Magic—Religious aspects—Christianity 4. Miracles 5. Occultism—Religious aspects—Christianity 6. Supernatural in the Bible

Dewey Decimal Classification: 248: Christian experience, practice, life

Cover Design by Jennifer Hanson

Edited by Adam Colwell

Contributing Editors: Kim Worcester, Marlene Moldenhauer, David Crosby, Greg Edmonds, Leslie Turner

Published by

ENCOURAGE
PUBLISHING
New Albany, Indiana
www.encouragebooks.com

DEDICATION

This book is dedicated to one of the greatest and most inventive illusionists of modern times,

André Kole,

a man who has guided countless people out of the darkness of deception and into the light of truth.

Unmasking the Masquerade

Contents

Section One

Section Two

Section Three

André Kole with David Copperfield: Used by permission

FOREWORD

André Kole

[For over a half-century André Kole has been widely acclaimed among professional magicians as one of the most creative illusionists in the world. He was named Inventor of the Decade by the International Magicians Society. Many of the hundreds of illusions he has invented are performed by the top magicians in the world, including David Copperfield, with whom he has collaborated on dozens of illusions, such as the disappearance of the Statue of Liberty. His tours have taken him to all fifty states and eighty countries world-wide. Having spent more than twenty years investigating claims of psychic powers, André is acknowledged as one of the world's foremost authorities on paranormal claims. Learn more about André Kole through his ministry website: AndreKoleOutreach.com]

Several decades ago I issued a challenge to all psychics and others claiming to possess paranormal powers, including but not limited to levitation or walking on water. If any one of the many thousands of them stepped forth and demonstrated their power under test conditions, I would hand him or her a personal check for $25,000. As if that tidy sum wasn't enough incentive, imagine the acclaim and free publicity to be gained by simply reading a thought, moving an inanimate object with the power of their mind, levitating, or predicting the future—without the use of trickery. I say "without the use of trickery" because, as the inventor of illusions performed by David Copperfield, Siegfried and Roy, Harry Blackstone Jr., Doug Henning, and countless other magicians, and as someone who investigated psychics, witch doctors, psychic surgeons, mind readers, and all manner of paranormal claims all over the world, I'd become adept at spotting deception long ago.

It's been over forty years since I first made the $25,000 offer. In that time, thousands of psychics have come and gone. Millions of followers have been duped by them, chasing a lie in search of the truth. Billions of dollars have been sucked from those followers' checking accounts. In that same time, I've publically exposed the schemes of many of those who claim to possess paranormal powers. But in all of those years, my resolve to handsomely reward and publicly acknowledge any genuine psychic was unwavering. Frankly, I wasn't too concerned about losing my $25,000, because I had seen so much deception passing for "the real thing." Regardless, I was still open to being convinced.

Now here we are, nearly a half-century later, and no one—no one—has been able to claim the prize. Surely, if in fact some people are gifted with psychic and other paranormal powers, someone would have stepped forward, demonstrated just one of those powers, and walked away with the prize money and the acclaim that accompanied it. But those who did step forward, submitting themselves to being fairly tested, failed the test.

Just one such test was conducted while I was touring Russia in 1993. An individual claiming the ability to astral project asked to be tested, hoping to win the $25,000 prize. I devised a simple test involving a boxlike cover placed over the individual's head and the sentence, "Billy is a boy," written in Russian on the opposite side of a chalkboard only a few feet from the alleged astral projector. The subject was then asked to project his astral body to the other side of the blackboard, read the sentence, and reveal it to the committee gathered for the test. After a few minutes the subject shared what he thought was written: "God loves us." Not a bad guess, since the claimant knew I was a Christian, but a guess nonetheless. I returned to America with my $25,000.

When I collaborated with David Copperfield to accomplish incredible feats like walking through the Great Wall of China, levitating across the Grand Canyon, and making the Statue of Liberty vanish, the impossible seemingly became possible to millions of onlookers. There were those who claimed that David had special supernatural powers. They couldn't fathom how anyone could accomplish such impossible feats without the aid of otherworldly powers. I've been accused of the same, despite the disclaimer I issue at the start of every show—that everything the audience is about to witness is only an illusion. Yet there are still some who simply are not about to be convinced.

The belief that some people have paranormal powers is ubiquitous, even in our "enlightened" age and culture. Hollywood and entertainment media have had a field day capitalizing and profiting from this fascination with the paranormal. Some skeptics claim that the prevalence of such beliefs is the result of religious teachings, and, ironically, as a Christian, I agree with them—but not in the way you might think. I do believe in the supernatural. But I also believe that God alone possesses the ability to perform the truly miraculous. What concerns me are teachings within Christian churches suggesting that some people—presumably under the influence of Satan—possess supernatural (or paranormal) powers. Bible passages are even marshaled in an attempt to provide credence to such teachings.

I find that many Christians assume, without really examining the biblical evidence, that Satan has far more power than God ever gave him and that he confers some of his powers to humans. But as I examine the Bible, I find that it lines up perfectly with the empirical evidence before me—people do not, in fact, possess miraculous powers that God reserves only for Himself. The Bible does tell us that Satan is the father of lies. Deception is his stock-in-trade. By deceiving us to believe that he is more powerful than he actually is, Satan's deception becomes a powerful tool for even more deception.

The three illusionists you're about to read—Rod Robison, Adrian Van Vactor and Toby Travis—put forth a convincing case that prominent beliefs in the paranormal are erroneous and without merit. You'll explore with them some of the history of alleged paranormal activities that were later found to be fraudulent or simply misunderstood. Some of these incidents had enormous impact on our culture and still do, years and even centuries later. You'll delve into what the Bible has to say about Satan's true powers and lack thereof, and how the scriptures have been misunderstood and even, in some cases, manipulated to lead people down dangerous paths to deception and unwarranted fear.

And you'll discover why Jesus, who has been accused by ancient and modern-day skeptics and critics of being a magician or even a myth, was, in fact, the One who really did accomplish the impossible, laying legitimate claim to being "God with us."

André Kole

Founder and Director, André Kole Outreach

Tempe, Arizona

www.andrékoleoutreach.com

ACKNOWLEDGEMENTS

A number of very special people contributed to the creation of this book. Several are magicians. All are magicians with their words, research, art, suggestions, and support.

Adam Colwell, Leslie Turner, Dr. Paul Simpson, Terry Holley, André Kole, Dr. Don Beirle, Alan Rasco, Michael DeSchalit, Dan Korem, Dr. Eric Chico, Scott Wolf, Elizabeth L. Hillstrom, Joe Turner, Greg Edmonds, Craig Greenwood, Donna Lamb, Kim Worcester, David Crosby, Marlene Moldenhauer, Devin Hanson and Jennifer Hanson (my incredibly talented daughter who designed the rockin' cover of this book).

I'm honored that the friends listed on the facing page have chosen to help underwrite some of the costs of getting *Unmasking the Masquerade* into as many hands as possible. Thank you each for your generous gifts.

I am very grateful to our beta team, who read, critiqued and gave an honest review of pre-release copies of the book. Your insights were invaluable and definitely improved the final product.

Special thanks to my loving wife and partner-for-life Jeannie Robison for her patience during my countless hours of research and writing.

Rod Robison

Ed and Jeanie Baggett

Wes and Rebecca Baker

Mona and Brad Beaton

Ron and Karen Behee

Sandy and Warren Bonesteel

Chris Bousum

Kathryn Branman

Scott and Charity Bray

Mardi Cameron

Eric Chico

Adam Colwell

Jed Crouse

Ed and Onita Davis

Ken and Barb Dewey

Pete Durkee

Brian Frank

Ted Gifford

Marganna Gillock

Craig Greenwood

Robert and Kathy Gurtler

Bob and Lynn Hanson

Fred Heeren

Sarah and John Herrington

Terry Holley

Gil and Becky Jones

Harriet Keith

Mark and Erin Lamb

Scot and Conni Lamb

Joseph Lamm

Rick and Sue Livingood

LaMont McConnell

Tom and Kari Miller

Joe and Julianne Muench

Mark and Kim Newhouse

Jim Ray

David, Bre and Owen Robison

Sigrid Ross

Dr. Paul Simpson

Cathy and Steve Skoog

Ken Sly

Marvin and Diana Sparks

Dana and Donelle Tison

Arthur Trillo, Sr.

Gary Trittipoe

Jim and Doris Tucker

Joe M. Turner

Thomas and Janice Van Keuren

Steve Varro

Phil Welliver

Tom and Kim Worcester

Section One

Unmasking the Deception

Rod Robison

This first of three sections traces fascinating stories from history into our current age illustrating our own vulnerability to deception and the sometimes humorous and often tragic results. Along the way you'll meet some of those who have claimed to possess the power to read minds, levitate, foretell the future, make objects move with only the power of the mind (telekinesis), and contact the dearly departed. Are those powers real? Are they simply cleverly disguised trickery? Or is there something, or someone, otherworldly hiding behind a mask of deception?

Rod Robison: Photo by Devin Hanson

About Rod Robison

Rod Robison is a mentalist, illusionist, author, speaker, and broadcast professional. His comedy mind reading show, "Mentallusions," has been a popular feature at corporate and organizational events as well as aboard Holland America cruise lines and at London's Magic Circle Theater.

A graduate of Cedarville University, after college Rod toured and recorded with pioneer contemporary Christian music band Selah in the 1970s. During those years he sang and penned lyrics for the band's songs, one of which, Fat Baby, was later recorded by Amy Grant on her million-seller Grammy award-winning album, Age to Age.

Following his years with Selah he helped found two Christian television stations in Ohio and Michigan before moving on to Christian radio in the late 1980s. Today he serves as Vice President of Development for the Family Life Radio network headquartered in Tucson, Arizona, where he and his wife Jeannie raised their five children in the beautiful Desert Southwest.

Rod's interest in magic was ignited nearly three decades ago when he saw a magician at Dollywood amusement park in Tennessee perform a trick where a copper coin transformed into a silver coin in Rod's own hand. Deeply perplexed by the trick, he lay awake that night obsessively attempting to devise a method by which the "miracle" might be accomplished. The next day he returned to the shop, bought the trick, and learned that none of his proposed methods explained the real secret.

That was the genesis of what years later became his popular "Mentallusions" show, during which he demonstrates what he calls "sleight of mind," popularly known as mind reading. Rod has been performing professionally for over 20 years and is a member of the Fellowship of Christian Magicians and the Society of American Magicians. Robison is often asked by audience members if he has psychic powers. His response: "It may look that way, but looks can be deceiving."

(Learn more about Rod Robison at www.unmaskingthemasquerade.com.)

Chapter 1
WHEN WEIRD THINGS HAPPEN

"All I want is the truth. Just gimme some truth." John Lennon

"What is truth?" Pontius Pilate

Before we take our first step on this fascinating and mysterious journey together, let me make something perfectly clear to you.

I'm a fake.

At least I am when I'm on stage. When the lights come on, the curtains part, and I begin reading minds, predicting the future, and making stuff move and float with the power of my mind, it looks to the audience like the real thing. Some swear it is. Others know intellectually that it can't possibly be real, but their eyes tell them something different. Because, well, seeing is believing.

Or is it?

But it's not real.

Like I said, I'm a fake.

I've seen the look countless times—that quizzical gaze from an audience member that says, "I don't believe you can do that, yet I just saw you do it. There is no explanation other than, well, you really are psychic. But you can't be, because I don't fall for that kind of stuff. Still, is it possible?"

It's called cognitive dissonance, a state of mental discomfort brought on by being confronted with new information that conflicts with one's beliefs or values. I'll give you an example.

I performed my *Mentallusions* show at a Christmas party for Raytheon, the aerospace corporation that designs and builds missiles and parts for The International Space Station and space shuttles. In fact, it was for some of their most talented aerospace engineers. I closed my show by floating a table around the room. Now, you can imagine the brainpower that went into overdrive in those moments. A room full of engineers faced with cognitive dissonance. A table clearly cannot float on its own without a power source and an aeronautic mechanism of some sort. And yet—

Immediately after the show, several of Raytheon's finest gathered around the table, "dying" to examine it. "No, you can't," I firmly assured them. Some of them put forth their theories. None guessed right. I don't know for sure, but I'm guessing that more than a few Raytheon engineers lay awake that night.

Being a mentalist and magician trained in the art of deception for entertainment purposes and having studied the deceptive practices of tricksters with more nefarious motives, I've grown skeptical of all things paranormal and psychic. I've seen and studied so much fakery passing for "the real thing" that I default to skepticism whenever someone claims to have special powers. At the same time, I am not a skeptical naturalist—someone who does not believe in a supernatural realm. I am, in fact, a strong believer in the supernatural. I believe that the facts of nature and the historical record of the Bible point clearly in the direction of both a natural and a supernatural world. You might call me a "skeptical supernaturalist."

As you read, you'll catch on quickly why I'm so skeptical of people's claims of paranormal and psychic powers. At the same time, I don't claim to have the final answer on all things weird and unexplainable. This book is not an attempt to explain every extraordinary experience or claim. There are other books that are more exhaustive on that topic than this one. I encourage you to read some of them, several of which we've referenced in this book. And to be sure, there are some such experiences that I don't understand. I'll tell you about a couple of them.

The Phoenix Lights

The first unexplainable incident happened just above my home in the Desert Southwest on the night of March 13, 1997. I happened to be out of town at the time, but some of my friends—skeptics all—witnessed a phenomenon that made worldwide news and was dubbed "The Phoenix Lights":

At roughly 7:30 p.m., a large number of people near the Nevada/Arizona border began reporting a massive V-shaped object the size of several football fields traveling silently and steadily toward Phoenix. It contained five distinct light-emitting spheres—two on each "wing" and one at the point. Others witnessed additional glowing orbs. Many witnesses testified that, as it passed over the clear night sky, the stars disappeared behind it, giving it the appearance of being a solid object, not simply lights flying in formation. Others reported that the stars behind it could be seen but took on a shimmering appearance, as though the object was translucent.

Over the course of the next three hours, it traveled toward and then over Phoenix, where it was witnessed by thousands of residents, and made its way to Tucson, where it was seen by hundreds more (including friends in my neighborhood) as it floated over our houses. Two of those friends were professional magicians and a third neighbor was an aerospace engineer. None of them believed that what they saw could be easily explained away. Another acquaintance of mine, a medical doctor, had what he described to me as a dramatic, unexplainable, even spiritual experience associated with his and his family's encounter with the object. The family was traveling north on Interstate 10 from their home in Tucson to a state swimming competition in Phoenix.

> *I have been a psychiatrist for twenty-three years, board certified since 1984, and got my private pilot's license in 1985. I moved to Tucson from New Jersey in September 1991. I have never observed anything in the sky that I could not explain until the night of March 13, 1997. We saw a row of approximately seven bright reddish-orange glowing orbs to the northwest at about 8:20-8:25 p.m.. . . . In an instant, the lights were directly overhead. While our car was traveling at about sixty-five miles-per-hour, they seemed to hold directly overhead for about five to ten minutes, still holding formation at about fifteen hundred feet.*
>
> *With the moon roof open, we could hear no aircraft engine noise whatsoever. . . . I was impressed by the perfect symmetry of these lights. With a good deal of time to observe closely, these lights did not seem to be connected to anything. It was as if the light or glow was the object. I could see stars immediately around a light and within the formation itself. From lead to trailer, the formation was about three hundred yards across. There was no evidence of a flame, ionization, or smoke trail. The light itself did not seem to be illuminating either an attached physical craft or object, or the ground. The lights formed no beams as a searchlight might. Altitude did not seem to change at all, and the formation slowly moved to the southeast toward Casa Grande. There were no obvious aircraft nearby.*

The doctor's description was fascinating. But even more provocative was his explanation of how the experience affected him and his family. After the lights passed, the family didn't talk about their strange experience, and their memory of it faded quickly. But a few months later, their memories of the incident flooded back:

> *During the intervening three months and since, our lives changed in some very interesting ways, all for the positive! Clarity of thought, concentration, and productivity increased. . . . I asked my wife about the lights months later and wondered why we had not stopped to*

watch. She stated very matter-of-factly, 'We were told not to worry, that this was not for us to be concerned about, that we were to keep driving.' She said that there was not a voice that said this, but that it was clearly communicated to her somehow. On separate occasions, I asked my daughter and then her friend the same question. They both gave the same answer without having talked about it with each other beforehand. I experienced the same communication. We no longer talk to each other about the experience. . . . I have been forever changed by it.[1]

They weren't the only ones who had a life-altering response to The Phoenix Lights that night. Several others had similarly profound personal experiences—including the governor of Arizona. A few days after the sighting, Governor Fife Symington called a press conference during which he ridiculed the incident, leaving the impression that he did not believe there was anything to it. Ten years later, during an interview with CNN, former Governor Symington admitted that he too had witnessed the object flying over Phoenix, stating it was "enormous." He continued, "It just felt otherworldly. In your gut you could just tell it was otherworldly."[2]

Symington acknowledged that he used his considerable influence to investigate, but to no avail. He reported contacting the commander at Luke Air Force Base, the general in charge of the National Guard, and the head of the Department of Public Safety at the time. "None of these officials had answers," Symington noted, "and they were perplexed."[3]

So what were the Phoenix Lights? I honestly don't know, which is not easy for a skeptic like me to admit. I do know, after studying many reports from eyewitnesses and proposed explanations by others, that they were not what many skeptics and some government officials who did not witness them claimed—flares dropped by the Maryland National Guard. Flares were dropped later that same evening, but the earlier event, witnessed by my friends and countless others, was manifestly *not* flares.

Other explanations that have been put forth include interdimensional beings, aliens from an advanced planet, Satan (an "angel of light" as described in the Bible), or an experimental technology developed and tested by the government. I discount most of the theories for a variety of, I believe, rational and studied reasons. But would I bet my life on any of them? No. I really don't know, and that's a healthy stance for a skeptic like me.

Speaking of skeptics, one of the most famous is my friend, internationally-acclaimed illusionist André Kole. He is widely recognized as one of the most renowned inventors of illusions in the world. David Copperfield, named by *Forbes Magazine* as the most "commercially successful magician in history," says Kole is "one of the greatest illusionists in the world today" and one of Copperfield's most trusted consultants. Kole is an investigator of claims of the paranormal and a Christian whose shows have taken him around the world for decades, sharing the Gospel through his incredible illusion show. In his book, *Astrology and Psychic Phenomena*, he states:

> *During my travels, I have searched out claims of the supernatural by investigating witch doctors, psychic surgeons, and others who are purported to possess amazing powers and abilities. Although my efforts to find anyone able to demonstrate legitimate psychic powers proved to be futile, I continued to hear and read stories of individuals who could levitate, read minds, speak with the spirits of the deceased, and accurately predict the future. Several years ago I began to offer a $25,000 award to anyone who could demonstrate to my satisfaction a psychic ability or phenomenon. As of this writing no one has received the award.*[4]

Yet even Kole had a weird experience he can't explain.

Asunción

Some years ago, André Kole wrote to my co-writer Toby Travis and me:

In the mid-eighties I left New York City to begin a tour of most of the countries in South America. During the following weeks I gave condensed programs and a Gospel presentation on national television in almost all of the countries. It was New Year's Eve and I arrived in Asunción [Paraguay] about 8:00 p.m., where I met my interpreter, who had just flown in from Ecuador. A missionary couple picked us up and took us to the hotel. On the way to the hotel, I remembered later that she told us that many people in the area believed that demons and evil spirits controlled the weather.

At the hotel, it was such a beautiful evening that my interpreter and I went to the roof of the hotel and prayed together at midnight as the New Year arrived. Following our prayer time we went to bed about 1:00 a.m. We were in a hotel room with a single bed on each side of the room. About 3:00 a.m. we were suddenly awakened by loud sounds and rushing wind going through the room. The most unusual phenomena were flashes of light like camera flash bulbs constantly going off. They were so bright I had to partially cover my eyes because of the brightness. I looked over to the other side of the room, and my interpreter was so afraid of what was going on that he had the covers pulled over his head. I got up and went to the window and observed an almost hurricane type of wind that was knocking over trees, along with this flash bulb-type phenomena going off all over the place. I got back in bed and tried to pray. It was as if a knife was cutting off words, and all I could do was stutter. I also sensed a force, as if there was a weight forcing me down in the bed, and it was hard for me to breathe. All during this time, that blinding flash bulb type of light kept going off all around me.

I eventually got back to sleep, and when I woke up in the morning it was as perfectly calm and quiet as it was when we went to bed. My interpreter, Libney, said he had never experienced anything like that in his life and had never heard of anything like that from anyone else. When our missionary hosts picked us up, they told of the damage that had taken place in and around the hotel area and spoke of the phenomena of the flashing lights.

Libney reminded me again about the belief of the people there that evil spirits controlled the weather. But then the missionary said, 'I have lived here for many years, and to my knowledge the only other time the phenomena that we experienced last night has taken place was about ten years ago[5]*—the night before Billy Graham started his evangelistic crusade here in Asunción!'*

That night we went on national television, which began our tour of sharing Christ with millions of people in the following weeks with one national television show after another throughout the continent of South America.

St. Elmo's Fire and other electrical possibilities have been suggested, but nothing came close to explaining the blinding light phenomena that took place in the hotel room and outside.[6]

Years later Kole asked Cliff Barrows of the Billy Graham Evangelistic Association team about that experience, which he confirmed. In private correspondence with Mr. Barrows' assistant September, 2016, I was sent these comments from his interview with Mr. Barrows about the storm in the fall of 1962 while the Graham Crusade was in Asunción, which mirror the memories of Mr. Graham himself. Barrows recalled:

There was, at the time, strong opposition to Mr. Graham coming to preach in Asunción. The opposition had arranged to drop several hundred thousand leaflets advertising their evening festival/parade to draw people away from the BGEA meeting that was scheduled that evening. As the planes were being loaded, the storm, with hail and winds clocked at ninety miles an hour, unexpectedly hit the city of 300,000. Planes were damaged, power was knocked out, trees uprooted, even the leaflets were drenched. Parade participants dispersed and headed for safety instead of blocking entry to the arena. The only location with power restored was the stadium scheduled for Mr. Graham's meeting. The storm cleared and, in spite of roads being blocked by fallen trees, several thousand came and heard Mr. Graham's message.

Mr. Barrows confirmed the bright flashing lights around the city, which he believed were caused by corrugated sheet metal being blown into transformers, but he did not indicate experiencing the internal lights and other phenomena Mr. Kole and his translator experienced. However, Mr. Barrows, like Mr. Kole, clearly saw the experience as a work of God to advance the Gospel, adding, "The power of God is inestimable." Cliff Barrows, who is perhaps best known for his work as the music and program director for countless Billy Graham crusades, his close friendship with Billy Graham and for his *Hour of Decision* radio program, passed away at the age of 93, just two months after this interview.

In his autobiography, *Just as I Am*, Dr. Graham also recalled the Asunción incident. He remembered the wind shattered the glass doors in his hotel room as he and others took cover, and the storm's aftermath forced the government to enforce a curfew on the city that night in order to curtail looting. They later learned theirs was the first time an "evangelical Protestant meeting had been held in Paraguay's five hundred years of history."[7]

In a culture permeated with belief in animism, such a powerful weather event that clearly favored the crusade deeply affected the response of the people.

In a later correspondence, Kole remarked that the seemingly inexplicable phenomenon he experienced was strikingly similar to an experience Jesus' apostles had on Pentecost as recounted in the book of Acts. The sound of a rushing wind inside the room, lights flashing, and the inability to speak sensible English words bore an uncanny resemblance to the day the Holy Spirit descended on Jesus' followers as a precursor to the beginning of the apostles' evangelistic "explosion."

Regardless of the time or place, in each instance, highly unusual phenomena played an important spiritual role. Following that fateful New Year's Eve event, God used Kole's tour of South America to win many people to Christ. After the Graham team's similar experience several years before that, his preaching of the Gospel saw many people won to Christ. Immediately following Pentecost, the apostle Peter preached and over three thousand became believers.

Was it an act of God, a coincidence, a natural henomenon—or something else? We may never know. But the thing to learn from all of this is that when weird things happen, we have to be careful not to automatically default to what our own bias may dictate without first examining the evidence. As Kole has said, "The unexplained is usually nothing more than the unexamined." Having thoroughly examined the evidence for all manner of extraordinary claims from the vantage point of an illusionist, Kole remains an ardent supernaturalist, as are my co-writers. At the same time, we remain highly skeptical of claims of paranormal power allegedly performed by people, whether Satanic or otherwise metaphysical in nature. As you examine the pages to follow, you'll understand why we believe this is the most balanced approach to take "when weird things happen."

Chapter 2

The Town that Talks with the "Dead"

"The essence of lying is in deception, not in words." John Ruskin

"They exchanged the truth about God for a lie. . . ." Romans 1:25

About an hour north of Indianapolis, just as you pull off the interstate, there is a little burg called Chesterfield, Indiana. It is hard to imagine at first glance that some consider this to be one of the spookiest places in America. Head west into town, then turn north a couple of blocks and you'll arrive at Camp Chesterfield, the popular center of all things psychic. Here is where they allegedly practice communication with the dead, known as spirit mediumship.

Century-old clapboard cottages line the narrow main street, most of them with signs in the yard heralding the houses' resident mediums and psychics. A massive tabernacle-style meeting hall punctuates the end of the street. Behind the row of cottages is a grassy park with a large meditative fountain, a quaint little white chapel, and a crumbling memorial to the world's great religious teachers. A turn-of-the-century hotel, New Age bookstore, and a museum dedicated to communicating with the dead complete an eerie picture of a place out of place in this quiet Midwest town.

Chesterfield was founded in 1887 when interest in communication with the "other side" was at a fever pitch. During a typical summer in its heyday, fifty thousand visitors converged on the camp for seminars, services, and séances. Many visitors came desperately desiring a word or two from their dearly departed loved ones.

Camp Chesterfield was still humming with activity by the early 1970s. Around that time, I lived about an hour west of the camp and had heard about the strange goings-on at the mysterious spiritualist center. A high school friend of mine and I decided to do our own investigation into the alleged paranormal activities at Chesterfield and planned our road trip. Though we were excited, we were more than a little nervous. Tragically, our joint investigation was never to be. My friend died suddenly in a car accident before we could make the trip. I took that as a sign that perhaps postponing the investigation indefinitely might be the better decision.

It wasn't until thirty years later, when I happened to be in Indiana on business, that I decided to drop into Chesterfield to attend a couple of their services. By then, as a professional magician and mentalist, I was well versed in the art of deception and knew that if deceptive practices were being used by the mediums, I would likely spot them. I wasn't disappointed.

I arrived with time to spare, so I wandered around the grounds and spent a little time in the bookstore perusing a few of the mystical and paranormal volumes on the shelves. Then it was time for the services. The little chapel in which the service was held was nearly filled with students anxious for their upcoming week of seminars on psychic healing, clairvoyance, and other New Age practices. The crowd of fifty or sixty people, ranging from young adult to the elderly, lined the pews.

The opening of the service was very typical of a traditional small country church, with the standard hymnal and people with their hands raised clapping along with old familiar hymns such as "Revive Us Again" and "In the Garden." If I hadn't known better, I would have thought I was in an evangelical church. But then the similarities ended. The special speaker shared her experience as a former Episcopalian who lost her faith in Christianity but found the truth when she discovered Spiritualism. After the speaker finished, it was time for the psychic demonstration.

Each audience member was invited to write on a billet (a small piece of notepaper) the first and last name of a loved one who had passed away and a question for the medium to ask of the deceased. Then we were to sign our first and last names and fold up our billets. The medium first placed three strips of masking tape over her eyes and then wrapped a blindfold tightly around her head.

"Blindfold billet reading" is a favorite trick still often used among spiritualist mediums. The billets are folded up and placed in a basket. The blindfolded medium then divines the contents of some of the billets, thus demonstrating supposed paranormal powers. The trick is very convincing and seems impossible—unless, of course, you know the secret. But here at Camp Chesterfield in a chapel nearly full of ardent believers in paranormal powers, it was an incredibly effective subterfuge.

On my billet I had written that I wanted to reach "Candy Robison," a childhood friend and cousin. I wanted to know if she had a message for me. Only about half of the billets got "read" by the medium and mine happened to be one of them. The conversation between the medium and I went something like this:

> The medium placed my folded billet to her forehead and in a rather ethereal voice asked, "I'm getting a 'Candy.' Is someone looking for Candy?"
>
> I called out, "Yes!"
>
> The medium said, "A last name of Robison."
>
> "Yes!" I replied.
>
> "You haven't seen this one since she was a little one, have you?" she asked.
>
> "Yes, that's right," I assured her.
>
> "Was she a relative of yours?" she asked.

> I answered, "Sort of. A distant relative."
>
> The medium affirmed, "Yes, she says she was your third cousin, twice removed. She says that she's doing well. Everything is all right. And she wants you to know that this week will be a new beginning for you."

I resisted the temptation at that point to tell her and the audience that Candy, my boyhood pet dog, had not been nearly that articulate while on Earth; but I valued my safety, so I kept my mouth shut. All of the information I had written on the billet was used by the medium to feed back a supposed message from beyond. Shortly after my canine encounter, the medium delivered a message to the lady sitting in front of me, allegedly from her departed father. Using the same deception that the medium used with my billet, she moved the lady in front of me to tears as she was led to believe she was in touch with her father.

At another service during my visit to Camp Chesterfield, a medium read two of my billets: one message allegedly from a still-living friend of mine named Ray and the other from Dante who, unbeknownst to the medium, was my pet llama. In all three instances the only specific information "revealed" was what I had written on the billets. Everything else was generic information, or in the case of the "third cousin, twice removed," dead wrong, if you'll pardon the expression.

I've seen the "blindfold billet" trick performed with and without the blindfold. I won't reveal the secret of the blindfold—there are several methods—because it is often used by legitimate magical arts performers. But the reading of the billets I will reveal because I've never witnessed a magician performing it—only alleged psychics out to deceive.

It's called the "one-ahead method," and there are a variety of ways it can be performed. For example, after the audience members have dropped their folded billets into the basket the medium takes one of them out, holds it in her hand, and, without opening it, "divines" its contents. Let's say that she says, "Who is trying to contact Hector?" A woman from the audience acknowledges that Hector was her husband. At that point the medium shares a "message" from Hector, which the woman in the audience is thrilled to receive. The medium then opens the billet to confirm to the audience the name written on the paper was "Hector." Then she pulls another folded billet out of the basket and does the same divination with it, and so on.

Here's what is actually happening. The billet the medium selects is one of two she is holding, the first of which she has already read and memorized. She either has concealed a fake billet and put a plant in the audience to acknowledge, in this example, the medium has successfully named her deceased husband Hector, or the medium secretly opens and memorizes one of the billets in the basket actually written by one of the audience members before "palming," or concealing it. Now remember, all this time it appears the medium has one unopened billet in her hand and she is supposedly divining its contents; but that's not the billet she is "divining." She is only pretending that the folded billet in her hand is the one from "Hector." When she opens the billet in her hand to allegedly confirm that it was, in fact, the "Hector" billet, she silently reads and memorizes the contents of that billet before palming it for the next round and showing the first billet to the audience. Now she's "one-ahead" on the rest of the billets, making it appear as though she knows the contents of each one of them before they are opened.

Don't be embarrassed if you have found yourself taken in by such methods; it can happen to almost anyone. A professional magician and hypnotist friend of mine, Michael DeSchalit, was, as a young man, caught in the grip of some members of Camp Chesterfield who started a Spiritualist church in his hometown of Tucson. The blindfold billet reading and other "spirit manifestations" performed by the leader of the church, Dr. Ireland, were astoundingly convincing—so much so that DeSchalit became a devotee. Ireland would invite skeptics from the congregation to join him at the pulpit, where the volunteers put silver dollar coins in his eye sockets then covered them with three alternating layers of adhesive bandage, tape, and cloth blindfolds. While he was being blindfolded, members of the congregation addressed billets to those who had "crossed over," along with questions they were seeking answers to. The ushers would then collect the billets in a collection basket to turn over to the ostensibly entranced Dr. Ireland, who had by that time allegedly contacted his spirit guide for answers to the congregants' questions.

Dr. Ireland then proceeded to receive messages from the "beyond," calling out names of the dearly departed to an eager and, sadly, deeply deceived congregation. If one of them happened to have slipped a twenty dollar bill into their billet, it was almost assured that their loved one would be heard from.

A few years later, my friend joined a local magic club and soon learned the secret to the blindfold trick and other tricks that had so easily fooled him and his fellow congregants. Today he is a successful performer using both hypnosis and magic to entertain audiences.

"During my time at the church, I knew nothing about the art of stage magic and I was seeking direction for my life," he recalled, "so I was ripe for Dr. Ireland's deception. Once I learned how a mere magic trick could be used to swindle others as vulnerable as I was, I became keenly aware of how someone with ulterior motives, a charismatic personality, and a few secrets of prestidigitation can draw people into deep deceit."

Chesterfield Exposed

In the 1960s when Chesterfield was brimming with the faithful, M. Lamar Keene, one of America's most successful spirit mediums, was a resident. Years later, he penned a book titled *The Psychic Mafia,* in which he exposed the inner workings of the camp and his own deceptive practices during his thirteen years as a spirit medium. Keene was one of the rising stars in the spiritualist movement and had a loyal following that made him a wealthy man. In his fascinating book, Keene tells of a network of mediums around the country that traded information about their clients. Thousands of such files resided at his headquarters in Camp Chesterfield. Throughout his book, Lamar tells how incredibly easy it was for him to fake spirit communication and phenomena that convinced true spiritualist believers. But was any of it real? In his book Keene states emphatically, "Every phase that every medium in the world demonstrates is fraudulent."[8]

Keene was able to dupe thousands of people with the most blatantly fraudulent practices. Why? Because his clients were so desperate to communicate with their departed loved ones they were more than willing to believe lies.

Every phase that every medium in the world demonstrates is fraudulent.

Frankly, during my visit to Camp Chesterfield, I expected more impressive demonstrations of so-called "phenomena"—something that was at least nominally convincing. But my brief experience at Chesterfield coincided with Keene's assessment of the followers of Spiritualism whom he duped for years as a medium at the camp. He stated in his book that his and other mediums' methods were astoundingly obvious, yet the mediums did not employ much duplicity. These desperate people were so expectant and so open to suggestion that it didn't take much to convince them. That certainly was the case during my investigation; it was eye-opening but disheartening to see a roomful of true believers taken in by such a bald-faced deception.

Ironically, the night before, I had seen the very same "blindfold billet" trick performed by an excellent stage mentalist who made no claims of special powers. His performance was fascinating, yet was presented in the context of mere entertainment. In the context of a spiritualist church service performed by duplicitous deceivers, it took on a whole different reality for those being deceived.

Although Chesterfield's legacy of deception stretches back over a century, it was an outgrowth of a massive movement that was birthed decades prior to the camp's founding—a movement that grew from a seemingly innocent deception by two young ladies whose ruse got more than a little out of hand.

Chapter 3
The Birth of a Magnificent Deception

"Oh, what a tangled web we weave
When first we practice to deceive!"

Walter Scott, *Marmion*

Camp Chesterfield grew out of the spiritualist movement which took the United States and Europe by storm in the mid-1800s. Spiritualism gave birth to would-be psychic wonders by the thousands. Its impact on Western civilization continues to reverberate into the new millennium but its flames were fanned by a tiny, apparently harmless deception one night in March, 1848 in a little town named Hydesville, New York.

For decades, that part of New York had been known as the "burned over district" because of the many cultic movements that had scorched the area over the previous several years. In a humble two-room clapboard house, two girls, Margaret and Katie Fox, ages fourteen and twelve, began hearing mysterious knocks on the floor of their upstairs bedroom. They summoned their mother to their room and together listened nervously as the otherworldly knocks continued.

Mrs. Fox, emotionally rattled by the experience, shared her distress with a few of her neighbors. Within days, word of the phenomenon spread across the countryside, and soon hundreds of the curious congregated at the Fox home to hear the bizarre rappings. A neighbor suggested a tedious but effective system by which the raps could be used as code to hold conversations with the disembodied entity, who by then had been nicknamed "Mr. Splitfoot" by one of the girls. The entity was more than happy to comply. As word of the mysterious conversations spread beyond the tiny hamlet, countless New Yorkers converged on the Fox homestead. "Mr. Splitfoot" was conversing with a steady stream of curiosity seekers and those wishing to contact their dearly departed, but always in the presence of the two girls.

Kate and Maggie Fox, Daguerreotype by Thomas M. Easterly, 1852
Missouri History Museum, Easterly Daguerreotype Collection

Within months the Fox sisters were a nationwide sensation. Their older sister Leah, being a shrewd entrepreneur, capitalized on her sisters' notoriety, instigating a very lucrative business by billing the two girls as talented spirit mediums. Only a year after the rappings began, the great impresario, P.T. Barnum, hired them to perform at his American Museum. Their renown took them to New York City and most of the major cities, then to command performances for Mrs. Franklin Pierce at the White House, Queen Victoria, the Tsar of Russia, and many other dignitaries.

The Fox sisters' enormous success spawned imitators by the thousands almost overnight. By 1852, just four years after the Hydesville incident, New York City alone had over one thousand spirit mediums. The next year, Cincinnati boasted over seven hundred. Within a few years, Spiritualism, the name attached to the movement, was the fastest growing religion in America. Congress was presented in 1854 with a petition signed by fifteen thousand constituents demanding an investigation into the mysterious happenings. By 1868, it is estimated that Spiritualist believers in America numbered in the millions.

All classes of society felt the draw of its magnetic charms. Even high profile celebrities like Cornelius Vanderbilt, Elizabeth Browning, Fredrick Douglass, Horace Greely, Washington Irving, James Fenimore Cooper, Henry Longfellow, and Harriet Beecher Stowe were attending the latest in-home sensation, the séance, where spirits of the departed were summoned by mediums. At least one dignitary, Benjamin Franklin, who had been dead for decades, was claimed by the Fox sisters to have visited their séance in spirit form.

Mary Todd Lincoln, President Lincoln's wife, hosted as many as eight séances in the White House in hopes of contacting her two sons, Willie and Eddie, who both had died in childhood. She reported being visited by each of them during these sessions. President Lincoln's involvement with Spiritualism has been long debated. He did attend several séances with his wife. But some historians believe he may have been there simply to lend support to her, as she was well known to be emotionally unstable. Ward Hill Lamon, a close friend and biographer of Lincoln's, stated that he "was no dabbler in divination, astrology, horoscopy, prophecy, ghostly lore, or witcheries of any sort."[9] It's not clear whether he actually participated in any séances.

He did, however, take his turn at debunking them. Lincoln asked Dr. Joseph Henry, a scientist and secretary of the Smithsonian Institution, to investigate the claims of a medium named Charles J. Colchester, who had performed séances in the White House. After Colchester gave a demonstration of alleged spirit rappings in Henry's office, the scientist reported back to Lincoln that the sounds came from Colchester himself and that he suspected trickery. The medium was later caught cheating and was warned not to return to the White House.

But, Mrs. Lincoln was an avid Spiritualist for many years. After her husband's death, she consulted mediums, including Katie Fox, in an effort to contact him. In her latter days, Mrs. Lincoln was judged insane and committed to a sanitarium. One of the medical judges who had her committed cited her deep belief in Spiritualism as both a cause and a manifestation of her mental instability.

As a hungry public craved more evidence of the exciting new "discovery" that the deceased could be contacted, phenomena produced by the mediums became more and more elaborate. Simple rappings gave way to table tipping, the practice of causing a table to "dance" around the room with the simple touch of the hands. Eventually physical mediumship developed, complete with floating props and materializations of the departed—all, of course, in near or complete darkness.

Even though mediums—even the Fox sisters—were being exposed on a regular basis, the public's taste for Spiritualism's promise of contact with departed loved ones seemed insatiable. Wars were especially generous to the mediums' business.

Thousands of young lives were destroyed by the ravages of the Civil War and the First World War. Both eras saw huge swells in Spiritualism's popularity.

Another contributing factor to the new religion's renown was a convergence of two social tidal waves sweeping over Western civilization during the 1800s. The first wave was one of spiritual anemia. Two centuries earlier, the Pilgrims and other biblically anchored settlers sank deep roots of faith in the New World's soil. Their faith in the reliability of the Bible had a profound effect on American society. However, the Enlightenment, a philosophical import from Europe with an often strong anti-supernatural bias, challenged America's biblical foundations. The miracle-working God of the Bible was seen as outdated by many Enlightenment thinkers. The promises of science, so some of the Enlightenment philosophers claimed, had made such a deity obsolete.

Some Christians hung on through the philosophical storm, anchored to their belief in a Creator who could work miracles and whose Word could be fully trusted. Others chose to follow the lead of those Enlightenment thinkers with a naturalist bias. Those caught in the middle who still chose to call themselves "Christian" at all found themselves holding onto a hollow faith in a Jesus who was a good moral teacher but little more: certainly not a risen Christ—and without the resurrection, Jesus had no more claim to absolute truth than any other popular religious teacher.

Blaise Pascal, the 17th Century Christian philosopher and mathematician, widely paraphrased as saying there is a God-shaped vacuum in every person that can only be filled with the Creator God of the Bible, actually described quite eloquently the results of spiritual starvation that marked the Enlightenment:

> *What else does this craving, and this helplessness, proclaim but that there was once in man a true happiness, of which all that now remains is the empty print and trace?*

> *This he tries in vain to fill with everything around him, seeking in things that are not there the help he cannot find in those that are, though none can help, since this infinite abyss can be filled only with an infinite and immutable object; in other words by God himself.*

By the early 1800s, a lukewarm Christian nation was beginning to feel the hunger pangs of that vacuum. Church membership was waning. The revivals of the Second Great Awakening swept in to help recover some of what had been lost by pointing the nation back to the primacy of God's Word. But many chose to fill the void with something that in their eyes was spiritually satisfying but less demanding than a God who called His people to personal accountability.

Having rejected the Bible's God yet deeply desiring a connection to something transcendent, Spiritualism filled the bill for multitudes. Its teachings spoke of a less personal, less judgmental deity as opposed to a God of love *and* justice. There was no finality in death, no hell to fear; only a crossing over to the next plane of existence, where the soul's evolution took it another step toward perfection. There were alleged "departed spirits" aplenty with on-the-scene reports to "verify" the existence of such a place. The consistent message coming through ostensibly from the other side was that all was well. The afterlife as described in the Bible was nowhere to be found in Spiritualist theology.

The other wave sweeping the country at this same time was the Industrial Revolution. Marvelous new discoveries and inventions were being introduced virtually every day. Many of them truly seemed like man-made miracles. Things that were only dreamed of for millennia—or never dreamed of at all—were suddenly reality. Just a few years prior to the Hydesville incident that gave birth to modern Spiritualism, the telegraph was invented. No one in human history had ever been able to communicate instantaneously with another person miles away.

It's difficult for those of us living in an age of instantaneous global communications to grasp how world-changing and mind-boggling this emerging technology was to nineteenth century people. Now the impossible was possible—and if the miracle of long-distance communication could be accomplished, why not communication with those whose souls resided on another spiritual plane? Suddenly almost anything, even communicating with the dead, seemed achievable. This optimism in science's miracle-working abilities was so profound that during Thomas Edison's final years, he was experimenting with a device he hoped would eventually lead to communication with the dead.

At the convergence of these social tidal waves of religious doubt and the emergence of science's new miracles, Spiritualism provided a seemingly safe harbor for those who longed for scientific proof of a spiritual reality. That is precisely what the proponents of Spiritualism promised. Through demonstrations of spirit mediumship within darkened séance parlors, life after death could be scientifically proven.

Or so its defenders claimed.

Chapter 4
UNHAPPY MEDIUMS

"Whoever walks in integrity walks securely, but whoever takes crooked paths will be found out."
Proverbs 10:9

In the wake of the Hydesville incident and its profound impact on America, Spiritualism's growth was unprecedented and—so it seemed at the time to both its proponents and detractors—unstoppable. But there was a fly in the ointment salving the souls of Spiritualism's believers.

By the late 1800s, countless mediums had been exposed as frauds. What seemed like undeniable spirit manifestations in the dark were exposed to the light of objective inquiry and found wanting. Even the Fox sisters, after forty years as Spiritualism's founders, admitted to a crowd of two thousand at The New York Academy of Music in 1888 that it had all been a sham. They admitted that the rappings that had snowballed into America's fastest growing religion were merely tricks. With Katie peering down approvingly from a box seat, Margaret even demonstrated one of the tricks by cracking her big toe joint against the stage floor, producing a popping noise for all to hear.

Earlier that same day she had signed a confession that was published in the October 21, 1888 edition of the *New York World*:

I do this because I consider it my duty, a sacred thing, a holy mission, to expose Spiritualism. . . . After I expose it, I hope Spiritualism will be given a death blow.

My sister Katie and I were very mischievous children and sought merely to terrify our dear mother, who was a very good woman and very easily frightened.

Margaret described in detail how their "rappings" were first created with an apple on a string, then later with their toes as neighbors began to come around and a more easily disguised method was needed. She continued:

And that is the way we began. First, as a mere trick to frighten mother, and then, when so many people came to see us children, we were ourselves frightened, and for self-preservation forced to keep it up. No one suspected us of any trick because we were such young children. We were led on by my sister [Leah Underhill] purposely and by mother unintentionally. We often heard her say, 'Is this a disembodied spirit that has taken possession of my dear children?'

That encouraged our fun and we went on. All the neighbors thought there was something, and they wanted to find out what it was. They were convinced that someone had been murdered in the house. . . . They went over the whole surrounding country trying to get the names of people who had formerly lived in the house. Finally they found a man by the name of Bell, and they said that this poor innocent man had committed a murder in the house and that the noises came from the spirit of the murdered person. Poor Bell was shunned and looked upon by the whole community as a murderer. . . .

A great many people, when they hear the rapping, imagine at once that the spirits are touching them. It is a very common delusion. Some very wealthy people came to see me some years ago when I lived on Forty-second Street and I did some rappings for them. I made the spirit rap on the chair and one of the ladies cried out, 'I feel the spirit tapping me on the shoulder.' Of course that was pure imagination.

Katie and I were led around like lambs. . . . We drew immense crowds.

> *Nobody has ever suspected anything from the start in 1848 until the present day as to any trickery in our methods. There has never been a detection.*

Actually, there were investigations made of the girls over the years that suggested fraud. As early as 1850, a physician examining the girls made note of the fact that the knocks always came from the girls' feet or from doors or tables that came in contact with their dresses. A year later, a relative of the girls admitted to assisting them in their subterfuge.

While in Buffalo, an investigation was led by medical doctors. Another one in Philadelphia was conducted by a commission of the University of Pennsylvania, followed some time later by a panel of professors from Harvard. In the last three cases, the girls would not, or were not allowed by their older sister, to cooperate whenever a crucial test was given. They were careful never to subject themselves to a reasonable test of their powers. The investigators did indeed suspect fraud but, due to the lack of cooperation on the part of the Fox sisters, were not able to document it. Margaret continued:

> *As far as Spirits were concerned, neither my sister nor I thought about it. I know that there is no such thing as the departed returning to this life.*
>
> *After I married, Dr. Kane would not let me refer to my old life—he wanted me to forget it. But when I was poor, after his death, I was driven to it again, and I wish to say clearly that I owe all my misfortune to that woman, my sister [Leah Underhill]. I have asked her time and again, "Now that you are rich, why don't you save your soul?" But at my words she would fly into a passion. She wanted to establish a new religion.*
>
> *I have seen so much miserable deception! Every morning of my life I have it before me. When I wake up I brood over it. That is why I am willing to state that Spiritualism is a fraud of the worst description.*

I am now very poor. I intend, however, to expose Spiritualism because I think it is my sacred duty. If I cannot do it, who can? I who have been the beginning of it? At least I hope to reduce the ranks of the eight million Spiritualists in the country. I go into it as into a holy war. I am waiting anxiously and fearlessly for the moment when I can show the world, by personal demonstration, that all Spiritualism is a fraud and a deception. It is a branch of legerdemain, but it has to be closely studied to gain perfection. None but a child at an early age would have ever attained the proficiency and wrought such widespread evil as I have.

I trust that this statement, coming solemnly from me, the first and the most successful in this deception, will break the rapid growth of Spiritualism and prove that it is all a fraud, hypocrisy, and delusion.

(Signed) Margaret Fox Kane [10]

A reporter with the *New York World* who was present at Margaret's confession described her demonstration.

But if her tongue had lost its power, her preternatural toe joint had not. A plain wooden stool or table, resting upon four short legs and having the properties of a sounding board, was placed in front of her. Removing her shoe, she placed her right foot upon this little table.

The entire house became breathlessly still and was rewarded by a number of little short, sharp raps—those mysterious sounds which have for forty years frightened and bewildered hundreds of thousands of people in this country and in Europe.

A committee consisting of three physicians taken from the audience then ascended the stage, and having made an examination of her foot during the progress of the rappings, unhesitatingly agreed that the sounds were made by the action of the first joint of her large toe.

The demonstration was perfect and complete and only the most hopelessly prejudiced and bigoted fanatics of Spiritualism could withstand the irresistible force of this commonplace explanation and exhibition of how spirit rappings are produced. [11]

What started out as a prank—one little lie perpetrated by a couple of schoolgirls—had, within just a few years, shrouded hundreds of thousands in a dark cloud of deception.

It is said that some time later the sisters, who had become penniless alcoholics in their latter years, recanted their confession and went back to their old method of making a living. Apparently, the "exposure tour" was not as profitable as mediumship.

Chapter 5

The Strange Case of The Psychic Odd Couple

"There is nothing more deceptive than an obvious fact."
Arthur Conan Doyle, *The Boscombe Valley Mystery*

"What the eyes see and the ears hear, the mind believes."
Harry Houdini

Some debunkers of Spiritualism's claims were men of science. Michael Faraday, a Christian whose numerous inventions included the electric motor, transformer, and the electric generator, also invented a device to test the spiritualist phenomenon known as table tipping.

By the 1850s, the practice of table tipping had become one of the evidences mediums demonstrated to prove contact with the spirit world. Two or more séance participants placed their hands, palms down, on a small table. Usually, after a lengthy time, the table would begin tipping and sometimes moving about the room. None of the sitters (clients of the mediums) were aware of any force on their part. It was claimed that the spirits moved the table.

Faraday's device was simple but effective. It consisted of two wooden sheets laid on top of the table with several cylindrical rollers between the sheets. The sitters' hands were then placed on the top sheet. The device was able to measure minute muscular movements called the "ideomotor response"—the same physical/psychological force that causes a handheld pendulum to sway, a dowsing rod to point, or a Ouija Board planchette to move. Because these tiny muscular movements are so imperceptible, it appears that the table moves by some outside force. Faraday's experiments demonstrated that the sitters were, in fact, unconsciously moving the table.

Lily Dale

A few years ago I visited a Spiritualist camp that was, for well over a century, considered "ground zero" for the movement. Although its heyday has passed, thousands of the faithful and the merely curious visit Lily Dale, New York each summer. While there, I witnessed table tipping for the first time. Even as someone who knew the secret, I admit that the experience was chilling.

Table tipping is not a trick in the normal sense of the word. It doesn't require a rigged table. Rather, in a very real sense, it's a trick of the mind. Typically, three or four people gather around the table—sometimes more if the table is larger—placing their hands on the table top. At times the group will sing; other times they summon the alleged spirits to assist. But always the focus of the group is on one thing—willing the table to move. It usually takes several minutes before anything "happens," and sometimes nothing happens at all to the disappointment of the anxious and anticipating participants. But often the table will begin to tip slightly—then more—then a rocking, rhythmic motion sets in. Depending on the excitement and unknowing cooperation of the members of the group, the table and its human "dance partners" are jostling around the room in a bazaar, awkward ballet.

What appears to the uninitiated as the table having a mind of its own or controlled by an other-worldly mind, is actually the collective effort of the group focused on the table moving. At the beginning of the session nothing happens because the group hasn't yet begun to work (again unknowingly) in sync with each other. As their combined mental focus "transmits" into a slight and imperceptible movement in the participants' hand pressure the table begins to respond and lose some of its balance. Once their hand movements begin to sync more and more, the table responds even more to the simple physics of the combined hand pressures.

Now, imagine what someone unfamiliar with the ideomotor effect—someone at least open to the possibility of spirits controlling an inanimate object—experienced when the antique table appeared to be dancing wildly around the room apparently without human assistance.

Later that day I walked into Lily Dale's Assembly Hall to examine the table. No wires. No mechanics. But the table itself was perfectly constructed to respond to the ideomotor effect. Its broad, thick square table top perched on a pedestal made it relatively easy to rock back and forth with not a lot of pressure.

Christine Wicker, a religion writer for the Dallas Morning News, recounted her own experience with table tipping at the renowned Spiritualist camp in her book Lily Dale: The True Story of the Town that Talks to the Dead. She visited the camp as a skeptical reporter in search of a story, but table tipping was one of her experiences that made her a believer, at least for a time. More than likely the table she used and described was the same one I examined in the camp's Assembly Hall.

> *Our table rocked the tiniest bit. Then it stopped…Then the table rocked again, left to right, left to right, left to right. Now it was tipping like a ship in a storm, up and down. Then it rocked forward and back, left and right, forward and back. We started to laugh with excitement. The table began to move in circles, hopping around like some crazed Cossack dancer. Our hands slid about on the surface. And then we ran, trying to keep our hands on the table as it twirled round and round, across the room.*[12]

That day she was convinced by her experience that something or someone transcendent had manifested itself in the table. And it rocked her worldview. But later that evening the reporter in her drew her back to Assembly Hall to closely examine the table:

> *As I stood over the pedestal table, I pushed on its edges. It was solid, heavy, and sturdy, not rickety. I placed my fingers on it and ran them across the surface as I had before, lightly and gently. Nothing happened, but as I kept at it, not cheating, just letting my energy rise, I applied pressure to one edge and felt a shift. I continued moving my fingers back and forth. The table began to rock. Now I was using no force whatsoever, just letting my hands slide and slip, and the table was bucking all over the floor on its own momentum, just as it had in class. Drat. The magic was gone. The mundane rules of the physical universe were once again in place. A top-heavy table. A pedestal base. Excited people. No spirits needed. We didn't cheat. Not consciously. Nobody had to.*[13]

Scientific investigators such as Michael Faraday and investigative reporters like Christine Wicker were not alone in their efforts to learn the truth, ultimately debunking the tricks of the trade within the Spiritualism movement. Many other investigations were conducted by magicians trained in detecting deception, both psychological and physical. As early as the 1850s, magicians were exposing fraudulent mediums by duplicating their tricks on stage. Yet, Spiritualism was not without its respected defenders. The famed scientist William Crookes was a staunch proponent, even after attending many séances.

The Cottingley Glen Fairies

The renowned author Sir Arthur Conan Doyle was by far Spiritualism's greatest public champion. However, Doyle's gullibility regarding fantastic claims was somewhat legendary. In 1917, two young cousins named Elsie Wright and Frances Griffith, in the tradition of the Fox sisters, perpetrated a hoax involving photos of themselves posed next to fairies dancing in a forested spot in England called Cottingley Glen. The fairy photos were crude fakes and the fairies themselves were later discovered to have been cut from a book of children's tales popular at the time. But that didn't stop Conan Doyle from taking the photos on a world tour, touting them as proof positive of the existence of fairies and convincing many attendees in the process.

In the early 1980s, Frances, then in her elder years, confessed:

Two village kids and a brilliant man like Conan Doyle—well, we could only keep quiet. . . . I never even thought of it as being a fraud—it was just Elsie and I having a bit of fun and I can't understand to this day why they were taken in—they wanted to be taken in.[14]

The fifth fairy photograph, taken by Francis Griffith.

Indeed they did. Even Frances herself fell victim to her own deception. In a recent correspondence, magic historian and author Greg Edmonds stated that, even later in her life, Frances insisted that one of the fairies was real:

You may be interested to know that I've also made contact with Frances Griffiths' daughter, Christine. She confirms that Frances

> *went to her grave claiming the fifth 'fairy photograph' was real. She finished her mother's memoirs in 2009. . . . As to her motivation regarding the insistence that there really were ethereal fairy images in the final photo (the 'fairy bower,' as she called it), Frances may have actually wanted to believe so badly herself, she was convinced she saw something that wasn't there. As my wife Tammie reminded me just yesterday, people see what they want to see.*[15]

One of deception's most ardent and enabling companions is desire. Conan Doyle and his fellow believers in all things paranormal had a driving desire to believe in the transcendent, but a desire often not tempered by an objective search for truth, regardless of where the evidence led. More on that later. But for now, let me introduce you to the "psychic odd couple."

Conan Doyle was fascinated by the apparent paranormal powers of world-famous magician Harry Houdini. Houdini was a fabulous escape artist whose feats defied explanation. But he made no claims to anything beyond being a very clever magician. The famous author insisted, however, that Houdini was able to escape locked trunks, jail cells, handcuffs, and all manner of constraints by dematerializing himself, despite Houdini's assurances to the contrary.

One of deception's most ardent and enabling companions is desire.

The relationship between the two men, though, was one of Spiritualism's oddest tales. They were fast friends despite the fact that they could not have been further apart in their opinions of Spiritualism and paranormal powers. Conan Doyle, the creator of the smoothly logical Sherlock Holmes character, seemed to be without Holmes' uncanny ability to sift through the evidence and discover the truth. Houdini, the most celebrated trickster of his time, had the training necessary to see deception where others saw paranormal phenomena.

The two celebrities spent many late hours discussing their differences regarding Conan Doyle's chosen religion. Neither was swayed to the other's beliefs, yet they remained friends for several years. Their friendship was eventually strained after Conan Doyle and his wife tried to contact Houdini's mother in a séance which the magician attended. Lady Doyle, ostensibly under the influence of Houdini's mother's spirit, scribbled a message to Harry. Houdini was disappointed. The message, which began with a crude drawing of a cross at the top of the first page (Houdini and his mother were Jewish, the son and wife of a Rabbi), was in English, a language Houdini claimed his mother never used when writing. In the supposed message, she referred to him as "Harry," a name she never called him because his given name was Erik. Harry was his "Americanized" name. To Houdini, this was not only a blow to his sincere desire to contact his mother—it was yet another proof of Spiritualism's true nature.

The wedge was hammered more deeply into their relationship when Houdini wrote publicly of his disbelief in Lady Conan Doyle's "spirit" message, and when he exposed the renowned medium "Margery" (Mina Crandon) whom Conan Doyle firmly supported. The former friends never spoke to each other again. After Houdini's death, though, Conan Doyle did continue to correspond with Beatrice, Houdini's widow, regarding what he regarded as favorable attempts by other

HOUDINI STIRRED BY ARTICLE, MAY SUE SIR ARTHUR

Noted Magician Is Angry at Creator of Sherlock Holmes for Published Attack.

NEW YORK, Jan. 27—Houdini, the magician, "contemplates legal action" against Sir Arthur Conan Doyle as a result of remarks about him contained in a copyrighted article by Dr. Doyle, published yesterday in the Boston

Springfield Union article Jan 27, 1925[157]

mediums to contact the late magician. None of these attempts proved to be successful.

Houdini, himself an ex-fraudulent medium, spent the last several years of his life searching for the "real thing." He sincerely wanted to contact his dear departed mother, if such a thing was possible. If it was not possible to contact the dead and the claims of mediums were nothing more than empty promises propped up by fakery, Houdini determined that he would make it his mission to expose them publicly—and expose he did. If anyone could discover the truth about the claims of spiritualist mediums, it was the master of deception, Houdini. He offered $10,000—a huge sum in those days—to any medium who could produce true spiritual phenomena. After years of attending hundreds of séances and tirelessly investigating the claims of countless others, the result was hundreds of publicly humiliated fake mediums. In 1924, he wrote a book about his investigations entitled *A Magician Among the Spirits.* In it, he wrote:

> *I have not found one incident that savored of the genuine. . . . I have said many times that I am willing to believe, want to believe, and will believe if the Spiritualists can show any substantiated proof, but until they do, I shall have to live on, believing, from all the evidence shown me and from what I have experienced, that Spiritualism has not been proven satisfactory to the world at large and that none of the evidence offered has been able to stand up under the fierce rays of investigation.*[16]

Houdini's exposure of fake mediumship probably had more to do with Spiritualism's decline in the early twentieth century than any other single factor. The public became wary of physical mediumship—floating trumpets, ringing bells, and materialized spirits that looked more like mediums wrapped in bed sheets.

Although its popularity was not what it was in the early part of the century, the religion continued to have a significant following even into the late twentieth and early twenty-first centuries. It had evolved through the following decades, and the public's taste for communication with the "beyond" had not abated. In response, the old movement merely mutated into something perhaps even more deceptive than its original form.

Chapter 6

PSYCHIC DECEPTION IN THE NEW MILLENNIUM

"What has been will be again, what has been done will be done again; there is nothing new under the sun."
Solomon, Ecclesiastes 1:9

By the mid-twentieth century, relentless exposures by Houdini and other debunkers had taken their toll on the old style of spirit mediumship. But a new form of spirit contact expanded on the old theme.

The term "channelers" was popularized by the New Age Movement, a loose-knit but highly influencial complex of various mystical religions that emerged in the 1970s. It has been described as "a combination of modern science and mathematical physics along with astrology, occultism, religious mysticism and nature worship."[17]

Channelers often describe those "contacted" not only as departed souls but sometimes angels, aliens, elves, and interdimensional beings. Unlike the spirit mediums of old, most channelers did not materialize physical manifestations of the spirit world. They primarily acted as mouthpieces of the disembodied entities. Consequently, they are more difficult to expose, since there is little or no physical evidence to examine.

By the year 2000, there were over one thousand professional channelers in California alone, charging anywhere from ten to fifteen hundred dollars per session. Actress Shirley MacLaine has long been one of channeling's highest profile followers. Her book *Out On a Limb*, which chronicled her experiences with her own personal spirit entity, created a sensation in the 1980s, as did her made-for-TV movie of the same name. Although the terms "medium" and "channeler" are sometimes used interchangeably, medium usually refers to someone who presumably contacts the dead while channelers contact a wide variety of spirit entities and are most often associated with the New Age Movement.

In recent years, however, spirit mediumship has made another comeback. Psychic luminaries such as Sylvia Browne and James Van Praagh acted as mediators between the living and the dead without the trappings of the old séance rooms. One of the more popular self-proclaimed mediums is John Edward. A former ballroom dance instructor, Edward's television program *Crossing Over with John Edward* (which rather appropriately aired on the Sci-Fi Channel from 2000-2004) was very popular for several years and, as a result, Edward continues to be hailed as one of the world's most popular spirit mediums. With boy-next-door good looks and an apparent sincerity to match, Edward wows audience members with a mix of lucky hits and specific information about their departed loved ones. His rapid-fire delivery of messages from beyond makes his presentations not only highly entertaining but very believable.

However, anyone willing to look beyond the façade will find that Edward is no more the "real thing" than his predecessors. He employs a combination of techniques including cold reading, which we'll discuss later, and very likely hot reading, or the gathering of specific information prior to his readings. Both are techniques commonly used by mediums. One rather telling bit of evidence indicating the use of both techniques flashed on the screen as the credits of his program rolled.

> *The Producer has relied heavily on the contributions of John Edward and other third parties in the creation of this program,*

> *which has been produced* ***for entertainment purposes only.*** *The materials and opinions presented in this program by John Edward and other third parties, including statements, predictions, documents, photos and video footage, come solely from their respective third party sources and are not the views, opinions and responsibility of the Producer and are* ***not meant or intended to be a form of advice, instruction, suggestion, counsel or factual statement in any way whatsoever.*** (Emphasis mine)

This caveat sounds like an attorney's disclaimer, which might be better interpreted as, "We received some inside information on the guests before the show, so don't take any of this seriously." The above 93-word disclaimer was displayed on the screen for all of two seconds—not long enough to read or disrupt anyone's misplaced trust in Mr. Edward. A "Hot Reading" Case in point: Joe Nickell, Ph.D., Senior Research Fellow of the Committee for Skeptical Inquiry (CSI) and "Investigative Files" columnist, referred in his *Skeptical Inquirer* article, "John Edward: Hustling the Bereaved," to a taping for *Dateline NBC*, during which Edward was caught picking up personal information from a cameraman and later repeating it to him during a psychic reading.[18]

Edward's show was cancelled in 2004, but he subsequently launched a new program in 2006, *John Edward Cross Country*, in which he continues to "hustle the bereaved."

Theresa Caputo, star of the reality show *Long Island Medium*, is yet another self-proclaimed mouthpiece for the dead. Journalist Jaime Franchi attended one of her live sessions, during which Caputo ostensibly connected with several audience members' departed loved ones.

Caputo threw out more questions to the audience, asking specific questions that, when they weren't met with nods of agreement, became described as merely symbols of other, more general things. For example, she asked a grieving mother who had lost her grown son, 'Why do I feel like you are holding him when he died?' When the woman shrugged, Caputo quickly covered by saying that that means he believes that she was always there for him.[19]

Caputo relies heavily on cold reading techniques, as do most mediums, fishing for someone in the audience who will raise their hand in response to an alleged message from beyond. Once that person responds, she asks leading questions to solicit more information, then uses that information to, hopefully, land a few more hits. When that doesn't work, she will alter the "bait" somewhat and move to another audience member.

Franchi goes on to describe Caputo's fishing expedition.

> *She questioned the surrounding people, asking again about a drowning. Then she announced that she wanted to speak with the mother of a young child who had drowned in a backyard pool during a party.*
>
> *The audience gasped in both horror and delight. This is what we had come to see. Yet no one seemed to fit the bill. A woman said that she lost someone who had drowned in river runoff, in about seven feet of water, and she wondered how, as the deceased stood about six-foot-four. Caputo shook her head. That wasn't who she was looking for.*
>
> *She approached the woman with the dead uncle again.*
>
> *"My uncle had a boat?" she offered.*
>
> *That wasn't it.*
>
> *"He built pools," the woman said, pointing to her mother. "He built her pool."*
>
> *That wasn't it, either. Finally the mother told Caputo and the audience that when he had died (of pancreatic cancer), his lungs had filled up with fluid.*
>
> *"Perfect!" Caputo declared.*[20]

After numerous misses, finally—she got a sort of "stretching-it-more-than-a-little-bit hit." Yet, many audience members still walked away convinced, remembering the hits but forgetting or ignoring the overwhelming number of misses. Desperation and grief can often leave one wide open to deception.

Sometimes the misses can be downright humorous. Shortly after the death of Frank Sinatra, I was listening to a psychic radio program interview during which the host and her medium guest were discussing various people who had "passed over" and whom the medium had channeled. Bear in mind that Sinatra had only been dead a few days and it was very big news in the media. The conversation went something like this:

> The host said, "So, what do you see for Frank Sinatra?"
>
> The medium answered, "Well, when he passes on, I'm sure he'll be welcomed on the other side."
>
> The host, sounding a little puzzled, responded, "But Sinatra just died a few days ago."
>
> "He did?" answered the startled medium.
>
> "Yes, just this week," the host responded.
>
> The medium, now sounding embarrassed, answered, "Oh, I didn't realize that."

Apparently, the medium's contacts on the other side didn't get the good news of Frank's arrival to her before going on the air.

But most adherents of spirit contact, whether the spiritualist medium or New Age channeler, take the issue "dead" seriously. Despite a century and a half of debunking, the belief in contact with the dead thrives. The number of television shows and movies based on the paranormal and, in particular, contact with the dead, escalated into the new millennium. In a 2005 Gallup poll, thirty-two percent of Americans believe in ghosts. An interesting side note in the study revealed that those who are more conservative ideologically tend to be much more skeptical of the paranormal than liberals.[21]

A 2011 study published by LiveScience.com showed:

- 71 percent of people in the United States claim to have had a paranormal experience
- 34 percent believe in ghosts
- 56 percent believe that ghosts are spirits of the dead
- 41 percent believe in extrasensory perception
- 37 percent believe in haunted houses. [22]

Much like the nineteenth century, today we live in a time of great technological and philosophical transition. The Information Age has brought us "miracles" of communication that have radically changed our lives. Postmodernism, a dominant philosophical worldview of the first decades of the twenty-first century, suggests that universal, objective truth is non-existent and that the only "truth" is one's own personal, subjective truth. When such philosophical changes occur in societies, the result is often a spiritual disconnectedness. But because that God-shaped vacuum Pascal referred to is a universal longing, people will almost always attempt to fill it with something. Often that something is a form of spirituality—an attempt to connect with something or someone transcendent—but one rooted in a non-biblical worldview. So it comes as no surprise that modern day Spiritualism, New Age channeling, and other paranormal interests are so prevalent.

Even though countless mediums and channelers have been soundly exposed as frauds and objective evidence of psychic phenomena is so often found lacking, the question that still haunts many is, "Could *some* of it be real?" Before we get too far into a discussion of what is really behind the manifestations claimed by practitioners of the paranormal, one very important point must be emphasized. The deceptive practices of mediums, channelers, psychics, and others of their persuasion have led millions astray. Whether those practices involve clever trickery, psychological delusions, or direct demonic intervention is not as important a consideration as is the fact that people are being deluded.

The deceptive practices of mediums, channelers, psychics, and others of their persuasion have led millions astray.

Deception is deception, whatever form it takes. Jesus said that Satan is the "father of lies" and that when he speaks he lies, because deception is his native tongue (John 8:44). Although it is important that we be aware of how deceptions are perpetrated so that we can discern truth, we should not lose sight of the fact that people are being led into a lie, regardless of the path that lie takes. If people are being persuaded away from truth—and they are—we can be assured that "the father of lies" is behind it, one way or another.

Chapter 7
The Cold, Hard Truth

"It's easier to fool people than to convince them that they have been fooled."
Mark Twain

Television and radio airwaves are crammed with any number of psychic claimants and tales of ghostly encounters. Take a look through your local major bookstore and you'll find hundreds of titles recounting psychic and other paranormal experiences by the thousands. An Amazon search of "paranormal" will yield tens of thousands of books, with many offering instructions on how to tap into occult powers. But how much of the mountain of anecdotal evidence is backed by objective reality, and how much might be deception, active imaginations, or even urban legend? If, in fact, real physical paranormal manifestations are happening to real people, especially in the magnitude they are allegedly happening, it seems we should be able to find several that can be verified under carefully controlled conditions.

For well over a hundred years, psychic investigations have examined claims of everything from spoon bending to remote viewing to foretelling the future. On the surface, some experiments seemed to be promising. But replicability, the ability to repeat the same experiment and get the same results over and over, has been a problem. As with any phenomenon being tested—whether psychically or otherwise produced—repeating the experiment under carefully controlled test conditions *and* yielding the same results helps verify the validity of the hypothesis. This rigorous method of testing and retesting helps eliminate such things as bias on the part of the researcher, statistical flukes, flaws in methodology, and even outright cheating.

Is that to say that unless an alleged extraordinary phenomenon can be repeated under test conditions, it never happened? To be fair, not all reported extraordinary phenomena lend themselves to being tested repeatedly. Some are, by their very nature, "one off" phenomena, assuming they happened at all. Yet those can still be tested in other ways, which we will tackle in our third section. But most psychic claims are those that can be tested repeatedly and in real time; if valid, they should stand up under test conditions. Taken as a whole, the history of testing paranormal claims has not been kind to the claimants.

In the 1970s, magician and psychic investigator James Randi trained two teenage boys to fake psychic abilities for what was known as "Project Alpha." They then offered themselves to be tested by a major psychic research institute at George Washington University. The researchers, unaware that the boys were cheating, tested their alleged abilities extensively and pronounced them to be genuine psychics. At a news conference, Randi and the teens revealed the truth, much to the researchers' consternation. One of those young men went on to become the famed mentalist entertainer Banachek. A couple of good lessons were learned from Project Alpha; scientists can be fooled, and even convincing "psychic" phenomena can be easily faked with adequate training in deceptive practices.

Many psychics, especially those who do psychic readings, rely on a technique called cold reading, the learned ability to "read" a person using various techniques involving observation and knowledge of human nature. What may appear to the sitter (the one being read) as information the psychic could not possibly have known may, in reality, be a product of cold reading.

Comedian and actor Steve Martin starred in a movie in 1992 called *Leap of Faith*. Martin played a burned out tent revivalist named Jonas Nightengale whose lust for money and power rules not only his life but his "ministry" as well. He employs a number of fraudulent methods to demonstrate his supposed God-given powers to small town attendees at his traveling show. He then "shears the sheep" of their hard-earned money and moves on to greener pastures in some other unsuspecting town. Despite its cynical opening premise, the storyline eventually develops toward a refreshing, redemptive theme contrasting the bankruptcy of a life focused on deceit with the richness of a faith in a transcendent God.

In one of the opening scenes, Jonas' touring bus is pulled over by a policeman for speeding. Before stepping out of the bus, Jonas bets his crew that he can get out of the ticket by cold reading the cop. With a country boy grin, the revivalist strides confidently up to the officer, only to find that he is about to have the book thrown at him. The cop is in no mood to be smooth-talked. Then Jonas begins to turn on the psychic performance. By picking up clues from everything from the cop's bitter manner to seemingly insignificant items in his patrol car, he weaves a convincing description of personal hardships the policeman is going through. Within a few minutes, Jonas has transformed a hostile law enforcement officer ready to slap a heavy fine on him into a friend for life. The officer even hands Jonas a donation as he thanks him for helping him see the light. Although the scene is somewhat fanciful, it's a powerful portrayal of the ability of a good cold reader to capture the confidence of his audience.

Dan Korem, an investigative journalist who for years made his living as a professional magician and mentalist, reveals the six basic techniques of cold reading in his book *Powers*. Following are the techniques and my comments on their use:

1 The Barnum Effect

The readers usually start with general comments that can relate to anyone. . . . Here's an example:

"Some of your aspirations tend to be pretty unrealistic. At times you are extroverted, affable, sociable, while at other times you are introverted, wary, and reserved. You have found it unwise to be too frank in revealing yourself to others. You pride yourself on being an independent thinker and do not accept others' opinions without satisfactory proof.'[23]

Numerous tests have shown that when asked which statement most accurately describes them, a Barnum reading or an accurate psychological profile of themselves, a significant number of people will choose the Barnum reading. A skilled psychic reader will not rely strictly on stock statements like the one above, but will customize the reading based on cues that the sitter gives him.

2 Identifying the Psychological Profile

"If the reader can partially pinpoint one's personality type, then it is possible to know the client's likely strengths and weaknesses."

There are numerous ways of classifying people according to their personality type. One of the most popular is the choleric, sanguine, phlegmatic, and melancholic characterizations. Once a person is well-studied in these profiles, it's not hard to figure out the category that fits for a person—even someone you've only known for a few minutes. Although this knowledge doesn't give a lot of specific information on the person, it can go a long way in customizing a reading.[24]

By being a good student of human nature, a psychic reader can surmise a lot of information about the person they are reading. Most people who come to psychics do so because they are concerned about one or more of three personal issues: money, love, or health. This alone gives the reader a fairly narrow field from which to begin a reading. Another way of zeroing in on a person's issues is by age and gender profiling. A woman in her early twenties is likely concerned about love while a woman in her late sixties is likely concerned about her health.

3 Physical Observation and Micro-Expressions

Useful information can be obtained simply by being observant. The manner in which a person walks into a room, their taste in clothing, the amount and type of jewelry they wear, their handshake, and a hundred other clues can be turned into information to feed back to the person during a reading. Micro-expressions are subconscious clues, especially in facial expressions, that the sitter gives the reader. By carefully observing the sitter's reactions to the reading, the psychic can tell whether or not she is on target or if she needs to take the reading another direction. Korem comments:

> *The sense of touch is commonly used by the palm reader. . . . What the reader feels for are uncontrollable muscle movements in the hand elicited in response to specific statements. The muscle responses are called ideomotor action. . . . A common practice by psychics who don't read palms is to place one of their hands on the client's hands, which are resting on the table. This effects a nonverbal display of empathy and also provides an avenue for receiving tactile impressions.*[25]

4 Accessing Specific Information

Also called "hot reading," the psychic reader accesses personal information prior to the reading. Online research and public files can yield an enormous amount of information on nearly anyone. I know of one reader who simply looked up the sitter on Google Maps to describe his neighborhood to him. Korem described a humorous but effective technique he used.

> *When I was in college doing shows to earn extra money, I would go in the men's restroom prior to the performance and sit in one of the stalls with the stall door closed. I waited until I heard a couple of men discussing something that would be of use later, like a piece of*

information relating to a business transaction. Next, I would note what color shoes they were wearing, follow them out and then match the voice with the shoes. Then during the show, I would have the person come up, select a card and then say, "I want you to concentrate on your card. Oh, by the way, that deal on Jackson Blvd? Don't worry about it. The bank will come through.'[26]

5 Loading the Language

When this technique is combined with the others already mentioned, one can give the appearance of never being wrong, even after an actual miss. Loading the Language refers to statements which can be interpreted in more than one way.

Let me give you an example of the type of statement to which Korem is referring. If the psychic says, "You're not planning a trip in the next few weeks, are you?" she is right whether the answer is "no" or "yes." If the answer is "no," then the psychic says, "I didn't think so." If the answer is "yes," the psychic has a "hit" and can play off of that by saying, "Yes, I thought so."

6 The Educated Guess

This technique combines the above techniques, narrows down the field, and then plays the odds so that the psychic can take some shots at specific information and come close or actually hit dead on. Korem recounts in his book a demonstration of pseudo-psychic powers where he did just that:

I singled out a woman from the audience whom I perceived to be very outgoing and probably of a sanguine temperament. The old saying goes that opposites attract, so it was a safe guess that her husband was somewhat phlegmatic—the opposite of a sanguine temperament. In addition, males that are phlegmatic make for good accountants, engineers, and architects. Because the majority of the audience were professionals, the probability was small that her husband held down a blue-collar job. I asked the woman to tell me if I was correct in my character analysis of her husband . . . watching

> *for any telltale micro-expressions which might tell me if I was on target or not. Her eyes opened slightly wider. . . which confirmed that I was in the ballpark. I concluded, "And your husband is probably an accountant—" deliberately not finishing my sentence. She nodded in agreement. I didn't complete my sentence, so that if I perceived a negative response, I would have finished, 'or an engineer,' as engineers are more common than architects. . . . With proper timing and hitting on the second guess, this technique can cover for an apparent miss.*[27]

You'll notice how Korem used a number of the six techniques to hone in on the target. He began with the observation that the crowd was made up of professionals. He then utilized psychological profiling to narrow the field down to a phlegmatic male by watching the woman's micro-expressions responding to his analysis of her husband. Then he took an educated guess at the most common professional occupation for a phlegmatic male, accountant, and got a hit. But he loaded the language, leaving himself an out just in case he was wrong.

Using combinations of these techniques, phone psychics are raking in the dollars. For years, television commercials touted phone psychics charging as much as five dollars a minute. Although in recent years court cases have discouraged television psychics from taking such a high profile, there are still countless phone psychics out there. You might remember seeing some of the commercials, where three or four psychics are sitting around a table talking to a person on the phone who is blown away by how much the psychics know about her. "You know that guy you've been dating," says one psychic. "He's married." The caller is flabbergasted. "How did you know?"

Despite the fact that the caller is obviously an actor (and not a very good one at that), millions of dollars are being poured into these companies' coffers by sadly gullible people. Beneath the veneer of the caring psychic who holds the answers to life's deepest mysteries is a scam that would have made the Fox sisters blush.

An acquaintance of mine (we'll call him Benny) for a time made part of his living as a phone psychic, and told me how he was recruited. A friend of his who was in on the scam called him one day and asked if he'd like to make some easy money. Benny, who is a talented mentalist entertainer, was given the number of a phone psychic recruiter. When he called the recruiter, Benny was asked to do a cold reading over the phone with her. He did and was hired on the spot. A few days later, his home phone began to ring with calls from people looking for answers to their personal problems. Since he was paid based on the amount of time he could keep them on the phone, it was in Benny's best interest to prolong the reading as much as possible.

You don't necessarily have to be a seasoned mentalist to get a job with one of these services. The *New York Times* reported that New York City's welfare department had entered into an agreement with one psychic network whereby welfare recipients were given jobs as psychic counselors. Did they need to bring any psychic abilities to the job interview? Not at all. The *Times* writer called the psychic network and was told that all that was necessary was a high school diploma, a caring personality, and the ability to speak English. The company then trained employees in the art of psychic readings. Some of these companies even provided their novice psychics with a manual full of scripts appropriate for any problem. Just turn to the right tab and presto! Instant cold reading. [28]

One little-known technique used by phone psychics is the sharing of information from company to company. One psychic hotline pays bonuses to psychics for every name of a loved one she can mine from the caller. This information is then stored in a database and traded with other companies.

Does all of this fakery prove that no paranormal experiences are real? As philosophers are fond of saying, a universal negative is impossible to prove. In other words, no one can prove beyond a shadow of a doubt that all psychics are fakes, since all psychics have not been thoroughly tested. There is always one more that *could* be the real thing. Within parapsychology circles it's known as the "white crow" theory. If someone claims that there is such a thing as a white crow, there is always, in theory, the possibility that a white crow exists.

In the same sense, theoretically, there could always be someone out there somewhere with real powers. However, the weight of proof rests on the person making the claim to demonstrate that proof. The evidence available from tests on those claiming such powers and the ease with which psychic phenomena can be faked, misreported, exaggerated, or misinterpreted certainly raises huge doubts.

Having said that, I do believe Satan can and does use deception to draw people away from God. After all, he is the father of lies—and he will use any means available, be it human gullibility, psychological deception, or physical trickery, to accomplish his task. Does that mean that there is no direct demonic involvement in psychic phenomena? I wouldn't go that far. The Bible makes it clear that demons have, at least in rare instances, possessed humans and manifested themselves through the possessed person's personality (Mark 5:1-20). So, at least in theory, some psychics, mediums, or channelers could be demonically controlled or at the very least influenced in some way.

One thing that seems to point to satanic influence within the world of psychic communication is the consistency of the message that "comes through" from "the other side"—through such occult phenomena as supposed alien abductions, séances, channeling sessions, and the like.

It's interesting to note that there is often a *common* theological thread that weaves itself throughout much of occult communications:

- The God of the Bible is not the true deity.
- Humanity is evolving into a higher, more enlightened being.
- God is within us all or we ourselves are divine.
- There is no sin, so there is no need for a Savior.
- There is no judgment or Hell to fear.
- Jesus Christ was just one of many enlightened teachers.
- Trust the entities sending messages from beyond.; they are here to help us.

The obvious anti-biblical themes that consistently emanate from the world of the occult point to the father of lies being behind those messages. In some cases, he may actually "speak" through some occultists. If the occult is connected in some way to Satanic power, does that mean humans have the capability of performing "miracles," or acts outside of the realm of nature, either through Satan or by the power of God? I have yet to see what I believe to be credible evidence that true *miracles* can be performed by humans, with or without the aid of Satan. Even more importantly, the Bible makes it clear that God alone possesses God-like attributes—an assertion that will be explored in more depth in the next section of this book.

Regardless of the strategic level with which Satan is involved in the occult, and particularly in the realm of psychics, mediums, and channelers, there are three reasons why God warns us against meddling with psychic deception.

1. It's a lie, and God is the God of truth. Why would you want to serve a lie?

2. Trying to find truth from the world of the occult will draw you away from God. You can count on it.
3. Deception, especially psychic deception, can be incredibly addictive. Many of those who have sought power or even comfort from the world of the occult have found themselves entangled in a deceptive web with no apparent escape.

God's Word, the Bible, should be our source of truth because it was given to us by the Creator of the Universe, the very Author of truth. He knows us inside and out—our weaknesses and our needs. He demonstrated His love for us by sending His Son to die for our sins. So when He says not to mess with the occult, we'd be wise to accept His loving counsel.

Chapter 8

But I Saw Him Levitate: Magician or Miracle Worker?

"People trust their eyes above all else—but most people see what they wish to see, or what they believe they should see; not what is really there."
Zoe Marriott, *Shadows on the Moon*

The reactions from the crowd ranged from awestruck to almost worshipful. None of the people approached by this mysterious young man expected to see the *miraculous* that day. But there it was. Undeniable. No doubt, most of them had seen good magicians do great tricks. But this was no trick. No mere magician could do this. Right there in broad daylight, on a city street in front of everyone—no wires—he just rose from the ground.

If you were one of the millions of viewers who saw the TV special featuring magician David Blaine several years ago, you may have had the same reaction. Watching this young man approach people on the street and do the seemingly miraculous was an unsettling experience for many. Instead of focusing primarily on the magician, the director of this special made the wise choice to focus much of the camera's attention on the reactions of the onlookers. Their facial and verbal responses to his minor and major "miracles" said it all: *Maybe this guy isn't just a magician. Perhaps he really does have supernatural powers.* You could literally see the cognitive dissonance and challenge to their belief systems that was playing out in their minds and hearts.

For several years prior to Blaine's success, magical fare on TV was limited pretty much to the annual David Copperfield special. Today, on any given week, you have your choice of several shows featuring magicians. Most of the programs are excellent. But the Blaine specials were indeed "special" because, unlike most magic shows, he wasn't just entertaining people. He was forcibly challenging his audiences' perceptions of the very nature of reality.

Not long after the special aired, friends and members of my audiences approached me to ask if I had seen the show. Some asked questions about whether there might be something supernatural—even demonic—about this guy. One friend stated emphatically, "But I saw him levitate!"

André Kole, as mentioned earlier, is a consultant to David Copperfield and has performed many of his own illusions, including levitating himself before stunned audiences. It's very convincing—so much so that some years ago a well-meaning woman in the audience stood and attempted to rebuke the demons out of Kole while he was suspended. Another misinformed Christian who publicly harassed Kole during a performance was a man widely regarded as an authority on the occult. He and his associates attempted to convince the illusionist to renounce his "Satanic powers" during a show in Germany. In his book *Mind Games,* Kole commented on the confrontation: "Here is a man that most of the Christian world looked to as being a leading authority on the occult, accusing me, a magician, of having supernatural powers. I was not able to convince him otherwise." [29]

I've had similar responses to one of the effects in my show, *Mentallusions*. At the close of the show, an antique table begins to move, slowly rises from the floor, then floats and dances across the stage. To the vast majority of my audience members, it is inexplicable and mind-blowing, but they know it must be a trick—somehow. I try to put them at ease by issuing a disclaimer that nothing I'm doing is paranormal, supernatural, or psychic in any way. In fact, I demonstrate apparent otherworldly powers to make the point that no matter how invulnerable we think we are to deception, we *can* be deceived.

Rod Robison's "Mentallusions" show poster

Despite my disclaimer and assurance that it's not "the real thing," occasionally someone will challenge me. Such was the case in Tucson as I was setting up for my show at a church. A woman walked into the otherwise empty auditorium and the conversation went something like this:

> "I attended your show a couple of years ago here at the church, and I need to let you know why I may not be in the audience tonight."

I paused setting up, gave her a friendly smile, and said I'd be glad to talk with her.

> "The last time you were here, you made a table float. I have to tell you that that sort of thing does *not* belong in the church," she continued, kindly but firmly. "That had to be done with some sort of psychic or satanic power."

She went on to tell me that after my last performance at her church, she met with the pastor to complain. "I nearly left the church over this," she stated emphatically. Her pastor assured her that I was not under the influence of Satan, I wasn't dabbling in the dark arts, and that every trick I performed was just a trick, including the floating table. But she apparently wasn't convinced. Thus her visit with me before my show.

> "So, was my pastor right? Were you really able to float that table without some sort of weird powers?"

I very, very seldom even hint at how I perform any of my mentalism or magical effects. But in this case, I felt the better good was to try to relieve her of her cognitive dissonance.

> "Ma'am, I'm not going to tell you how I floated the table. But I will tell you this. I could explain it to you in thirty seconds and you would immediately slap your hand on your forehead and exclaim, 'Are you kidding me? That's how it's done?'" She seemed at least a bit relieved, thanked me, and exited. I looked for her that evening in the audience but didn't see her. Maybe she didn't want to take any chances.

In 2013, a British magician with the stage name Dynamo stunned the United Kingdom and subsequently millions worldwide who watched one of his illusions on YouTube when he levitated next to a moving bus. Despite his method being apparent to seasoned magicians, many laypeople saw a miracle—including a pastor who wrote an article in *The Christian Post* denouncing Dynamo and other magicians for tapping demonic powers. As his article gained online viral momentum, particularly by non-Christians scoffing at his naivety, Christian magicians responded. One of those magicians was Joe M. Turner, president of the International Brotherhood of Magicians, the largest organization of magicians in the world. He's also a Christian and deacon in his church. Mr. Turner's op-ed response included the following:

> *I can safely assure you that the illusions you see performed in the various 'magical arts'—including feats by magicians, mentalists, illusionists, etc.—involve absolutely no connection to demons or the occult.*
>
> *"What those feats do require is a lot of practice, some fine motor skills, the cognitive ability to translate written instructions into physical choreography, and a sense of showmanship. The instructions in magic books, far from being arcane incantations of spells and conjured spirits, are mostly a mind-numbingly dull collection of instructions on how to secretly hold and move things with your hands. You'll also find a smattering of science and math principles, some interesting applications of technology, and some of the same self-absorbed navel-gazing you find in lots of other arts, crafts, and hobby publications. . . .*
>
> *. . .[T]he initial event described in Mr. Delzell's article was his experience of an illusion, apparently via a video recording. He watched a video of Dynamo apparently levitating during a stunt in London, didn't know how it was done, and assumed that it was a 'legit' demonstration of supernatural power. He went on to assert that such levitations are commonplace, along with casting of spells to conjure the power to perform such feats. None of those claims were documented.*

> *Instead of researching something that he didn't understand, Mr. Delzell chose to assume not only that the illusion was supernatural, but that the performer was in league with the devil. Rather than talk to any illusionist, or specifically a Christian performer, he went directly to accusations of witchcraft and contact with evil spirits, and the presumption that the art of magic is a gateway to demonic involvement*
>
> *In a world where Christians and the church are—often rightfully—criticized for lack of intellectual rigor, this kind of unnecessary incident does nothing to elevate Christ."* [30]

Dan Korem adds that "when people see a demonstration of alleged psychic or supernatural power for which they have no explanation *and* which has been presented in a *context as if it is a real power*, most people conclude that there isn't any natural explanation. My experience is that a person must *actually* see what, where, and how trickery has been done before they will be convinced otherwise." [31]

In 2014, a series of YouTube videos emerged featuring clips of various magicians, most of them well-known, in an attempt to "prove" that many magicians tap demonic powers to accomplish their mysterious feats. What proof is cited? The author of the series of videos points to the impossibility of the effects and the sinister persona of the magicians. To be sure, some of the magicians in the videos do sport ominous—and sometimes downright creepy—guises to enhance the mystery experience. After all, they are on stage playing a part.

As for the impossibility of the effects cited as proof positive of demonic aid, I can assure you they are tricks. Really good tricks—but tricks nonetheless. The secrets are *much* more mundane than marshalling the forces of darkness; some, such as one of the levitation examples, use methods that have been commonly used for well over a century.

.Satan gets far too much credit and free publicity from thousands of sincere but misinformed people in God's Church.

Sadly, tens of millions of views and thousands of comments to this video series indicate that many viewers have accepted the false notion that Satan's powers are far greater than the powers God bestowed on him, and have affirmed in the minds of non-Christians, who see the folly of the author's claims, that Christians are backward-thinking pinheads lacking any reasoning ability.

There have been many other modern-day reports within Christian circles of people with alleged supernatural powers. A popular spiritual warfare author recounted the story he received from a man in India who claimed to witness a shaman levitating over a crowd of onlookers. His and other popular books, both Christian and non-Christian, are filled with anecdotal accounts of apparent supernatural powers performed by people. A few years ago, a professor at a well-known conservative evangelical seminary taught his students that such a miraculous feat was witnessed by another seminary professor while in Ethiopia. But when Christian researcher and illusionist Terry Holley tracked down the "witness," he stated that the story was "greatly levitated" and that no such feat had taken place.

Holley recalled another such story that was recounted in a widely distributed book. This time the claim was that Tibetan monks had been seen levitating several feet off the ground. When Holley contacted the writer to get documentation, the writer admitted that the alleged levitations had not actually been witnessed by him but had been hearsay and, in fact, the account had been added to the book by a ghostwriter.[32]

But have *all* claims of such powers been disproved? Not at all. It would be impossible to verify or disprove every claim. However, the old adage, "extraordinary claims require extraordinary proof," must be kept in mind by anyone evaluating claims of superhuman powers. As pointed out by Holley, "it is not so much the *quantity* but rather the *quality* of evidence that is important." [33]

Many claims of superhuman powers have, however, been thoroughly investigated and come up lacking. Kole has conducted extensive investigations of claims of paranormal powers around the globe from his perspective as an illusionist. He has "looked for evidence of genuine ESP, psychokinesis [mind over matter], prophecy, psychic healing, and levitation. . . and has found none." But what he has concluded "is that every verifiable instance was composed of clever tricks—magical effects being presented as supernatural phenomena." [34] He makes this statement in his book *Mind Games:* "The unexplained is usually nothing more than the unexamined." [35]

One of the most celebrated levitations in history was performed in 1868 during a séance by spiritualist medium D.D. Home. He reportedly floated out of a third story window and back into another in front of three friends. Upon further investigation, the details of the witnesses' stories did not corroborate the claim. And, as with most séances, the lights were dimmed, bringing into question what the men were really able to see. In addition, some who had investigated Home reported that he was adept at suggestion and hypnotism. Yet, to this day, spiritualists point to this one event as evidence of human supernatural powers. Sir Arthur Conan Doyle even cited the Home incident as one of the convincing "proofs" that led him to embrace spiritualism. [36]

So what about all of those people who saw David Blaine levitate or refer to his other great feats? As an illusionist sworn to secrecy, I very rarely reveal to non-magicians how tricks are done. Why? Because many are the intellectual property of the inventor. Also, when a trick's method is revealed, the trick and the magician performing it are robbed of the mystery that makes the trick valuable to the magician. So, I won't reveal David Blaine's tricks, but I can tell you that most if not all of the methods he utilizes are commonly known among professional magicians. What made them look so real was not the methods Blaine used, but his marvelous presentation. People believed that what they witnessed were real miracles because he presented them as real. He didn't approach those on the street and say, "Hi, I'm a magician. Want to see a cool trick?" He simply demonstrated some really strange things that he, ostensibly, didn't even understand himself. Combine Blaine's very convincing persona with his considerable talent as a magician and the magic of video editing, and you have the makings of a modern-day shaman.

Former occultist John Anderson, who performed many apparent miracles in his role as the leader of a Los Angeles occult group known as the Blood Order, stated this in his book, *Psychic Phenomena Unveiled:*

> *In all the years of my involvement in the occult, I never was a witness to even one piece of true paranormal activity. I saw many things that I believed were of supernatural power, but all were later proven false. I have thoroughly researched the issue and collected letters and statements from many of the individuals involved. It is my conviction that Satan gets far too much credit and free publicity from thousands of sincere but misinformed people in God's Church. What is demonic is the power of suggestion that usually accompanies the performance, the lie that you can develop the 'God Power' within. This type of deception leads people away from the Jesus Christ of the Bible, causing them to focus their attention on themselves.*[37]

Chapter 9

But What About the Magicians in the Bible?

"When he lies, he speaks his native language, for he is a liar and the father of lies."
Jesus of Nazareth, *John 8:44*

In Chapter 2 of the Old Testament book of Daniel, King Nebuchadnezzar was awakened by a troubling dream. He was so upset by the nightmare that he immediately summoned his top magicians, enchanters, sorcerers, and astrologers to consult with him.

> *"I have had a dream that troubles me and I want to know what it means," he demanded of them.*
>
> *"O king, live forever! Tell your servants the dream, and we will interpret it," they replied.*

You can imagine what the king must have thought at that point. Maybe something like, *If they're such great miracle workers, why don't they just tell me themselves what my dream was? Why would I have to tell them? They should be able to read my mind.* The king's terse reply let them know that he was, in fact, on to their tricks.

"This is what I have firmly decided," he angrily shot back. "If you do not tell me what my dream was and interpret it, I will have you cut into pieces and your houses turned into piles of rubble."

Then he added this enticing incentive. "But if you tell me the dream and explain it, you will receive from me gifts and rewards and great honor."

If any one of them could have, at that point, told the king the details of his dream, he surely would've stepped forward. But no one did. In one last gasp effort to placate the king, they replied, "Let the king tell his servants the dream, and we will interpret it."

Of course, they knew that they had no ability to tell the king the details of his dream. Nebuchadnezzar knew it, too.

"You have conspired to tell me misleading and wicked things," he said. "Tell me the dream and I will know that you can interpret it for me."

They sheepishly responded, "There is not a man on Earth who can do what the king asks." Even under penalty of death, none of them were able to do the real thing. They came clean only when they knew there was no other recourse.

Even the "miracle workers" admitted that no man can read another man's mind. What an opportunity for Satan to have demonstrated his powers by reading the king's mind. But he didn't—because he couldn't.

In 1 Kings 18, there is another telling account of the contest between Elijah and the prophets of Baal. If ever there were an opportunity for Satan to demonstrate miraculous powers, this would have been it. Elijah challenged, even dared, the false prophets to beseech their god Baal to rain down fire on a prepared altar—and why not? Baal was known as the "god of fire." Mount Carmel, the location of this showdown, was the holy mountain of Baal worshipers.

Yet after hours of chanting, nothing happened. Then Elijah began to taunt them. "Shout louder," he suggested sarcastically. "Surely he is a god! Perhaps he is deep in thought, or busy, or traveling.

Maybe he is sleeping and must be awakened." Out of desperation, Baal's prophets shouted even louder, slashing themselves with swords and spears for hours, shedding their blood in an effort to appease their god.

Nothing happened.

Then Elijah prepared his own altar to the one true God. He had gallons of water poured over the sacrifice and then beseeched God to rain down fire as a miraculous sign. The altar was immediately consumed by a fiery display—a poignant reminder to Israel, and a warning to the worshipers of Baal, of God's incomparable power.

Another example is the encounter of Moses and Aaron with the magicians in the Pharaoh's court. To demonstrate the authenticity of His message, God instructed Moses to throw down his staff, and it would change to a snake. Pharaoh then summoned wise men and sorcerers, and the Egyptian magicians also did the same things by their secret arts: Each one threw down his staff and it became a snake. But Aaron's staff swallowed up their staffs (Exodus 7:10-12).

But did they really perform a miracle? In his book, *Powers: Testing the Psychic and Supernatural,* Dan Korem described the means by which the magicians could have counterfeited God's miracles on a smaller scale. Turning a rod into a snake, for instance, is easily accomplished by the same method modern day magicians turn a cane into a flower or handkerchief. [38]

I've personally witnessed the cane-to-snake trick performed by my good friend, magician Allan Rasco. We were performing a show together for a youth event. Rasco recounted the story in Exodus, then said, "I am fairly certain that what I'm about to show you folks is along the exact same lines as how they probably did their trickery." An assistant handed him a cane. Rasco twirled it like a baton and handed it back to the assistant. Facing the audience and showing his left hand completely empty, he then took the cane back from the assistant. The moment he grabbed the cane's midsection it instantly turned into a *real* snake. Rasco walked to the front row and allowed the audience an up-close and personal look at the wriggling black serpent.

In his manuscript, *Paranormal Lies and Wonders*, Dr. Toby A. Travis, one of the three investigators in this book, makes this astute observation about the other "miracles" performed by the court magicians:

> *As you recall, even though the magicians lost their pet snakes that day, Pharaoh was not too impressed and sent Moses and Aaron on their way. The Lord then told Moses to strike Egypt with what would be the first of ten plagues. This plague devastated the watery pride of Egypt when the Nile River was turned into blood. Again, the magicians created an illusion that appeared to duplicate the work of Moses. Of course, there was a large supply of blood around now for them to use. And it would not take too much ingenuity to figure out a way to spoil a bowl full, or even a pond full, of fresh water with blood. After the magicians had appeased Pharaoh with their demonstration, the Lord then brought on a plague of frogs that overtook the land. Again, but for the last time, the magicians also presented an illusion of producing frogs. But notice as you read the account in Exodus that after the frog production, the magicians were at a loss to create illusions that duplicated the mighty hand of God. An overwhelming infestation of gnats was plague number three.*[39]

Korem adds, "Logically, if the magicians had used supernatural powers to create frogs, a far more complex creature than a gnat, then they should have been able to conjure up gnats or flies, which were the fourth plague. Something just doesn't seem right here."[40]

Travis continues, "Something doesn't seem right because creating illusions to represent the first two plagues on a small scale is relatively easy to conceive using the tools of the magicians' trade. How many times have you seen a magic show today where the magician produces a box full of flowers, or a previously large empty Plexiglas box that instantly produces a pretty girl or a six hundred pound Bengal tiger? How much easier it would be to produce a bunch of frogs. But when the gnats come along you are talking about a completely different animal literally and figuratively. How do you capture gnats? Keep them alive until just the moment you need them? Contain them in a sealed secret hiding place and then release them on cue? It would be no easy trick."[41] It's interesting to note that after the plague of gnats, even Pharaoh's magicians admitted, at their own peril, "This is the finger of God."

In the New Testament, there are two magicians described. Both cases have been used by some to offer proof of supernatural powers ascribed to men. The first is Simon the Sorcerer. Acts Chapter 8 tells us he amazed the citizens of Samaria, who called him the "Great Power." He obviously had quite a reputation. The Greek word *mageuo*, used to describe what he performed, simply indicates that he practiced magic and does not suggest any supernatural powers. It appears from the text that Simon was just a good magician who passed himself off as someone who had powers.

The other was named Elymas the sorcerer. The account of his encounter with Barnabas and Paul is found in Acts Chapter 13. The word rendered "sorcerer" is *magos* and only suggests that he was considered a "wise man" in the same sense as were the magi that visited Jesus in Bethlehem when he was a toddler. Elymas is also called a *pseudoprophetes* or false prophet. Paul rebuked Elymas and accused him of deceit and trickery, but did not suggest any miraculous powers.

Second Thessalonians 2:9 states that when the Antichrist comes on the scene, "This man will come to do the work of Satan with counterfeit power and signs and miracles." Note that Satan's own right-hand man of the end times will only be able to perform deception, not miracles.

Another source of confusion regarding whether or not Satan has miraculous powers centers on the Greek and Hebrew words translated in some versions as "miracle." In reality, our English word "miracle," with all of its supernatural connotations, does not exist in Hebrew and Greek. For instance, the Greek word *semeia* is translated in Revelation 13:13 as "miraculous signs" performed by one of the beasts of the end times.

Is all of this to suggest that Satan has no powers? The Bible is quite clear that he does possess powers, but that they are greatly limited by God and do not even approach God's ability to do the truly miraculous. However, Christians need to be aware of Satan's power to tempt, incite division, and distract us from God. We are told in Ephesians Chapter 6 to "put on the whole armor of God" so that we won't fall into Satan's schemes. But nowhere in the Bible are we told that Satan has the ability to give humans supernatural powers.

Why is this distinction important? Throughout Scripture and in our present time, there have been many who have claimed to have supernatural powers. It is a deceptive seduction to think that we can share powers God reserves only for Himself. From the time of Eve, humans have been taken in by Satan's lie that we can "be like God." New Age gurus hold out promises of supernatural powers like levitation to would-be gods. Even some Christian teachers, popularized on television, offer their followers the promise of performing the miracles of Jesus and becoming "little gods" by speaking the right words in faith or "speaking into existence" desired things and circumstances.

Christians need to be aware of Satan's power to tempt, incite division, and distract us from God.

One of Satan's greatest powers is the power to deceive people—even Christians who should know better. By ascribing more power to Satan than God has given him, we allow ourselves to be fooled into fearing him. If we believe that Satan can make people levitate and display all manner of supernatural manifestations, then his power to intimidate us is greatly increased. We unwittingly become more vulnerable to his lying schemes.

Jesus unmasked Satan when he said in John Chapter 8, "He was a murderer from the beginning, not holding to the truth, for there is no truth in him. When he lies he speaks his native language, for he is a liar and the father of lies." Satan is a much better liar than he is a miracle worker. In 2 John 4:1 we are admonished not to believe every spirit, but "test the spirits to see whether they are from God, because many false prophets have gone out into the world." We would be well-served, then, to understand the truth about the limits of Satan's power and the limitless power of the Creator God.

Chapter 10

A Devilish Delusion

"But whatsoever is reported or conceived of such maner of witchcrafts, I dare avow to be false and fabulous. . . neither is there any mention made of these kind of witches in the Bible."
Reginald Scot, *The Discoverie of Witchcraft* (1584)

Through the centuries and into our current age, folklore and popular, fanciful, Hollywood-esque notions of Satan have crept into our cultural ethos, often supplanting scriptural descriptions of him and his powers. When we, even inadvertently, assign to Satan more power than he has, we give him more power over our lives.

Understanding Satan's true role in our world has been controversial within the Christian Church for centuries. To some, he's an innocuous, impersonal entity representative of evil, not someone to be feared or even concerned about. At the other extreme are those who see Satan as the force behind all manner of apparent paranormal phenomena from alien abductions to psychic experiences to ghostly encounters and even unpleasant natural phenomena such as bad weather.

Finding the biblical balance somewhere within that spectrum can be a challenge. Although the Bible doesn't dwell on Satan's powers, it certainly gives us enough information to help us draw a reasonably accurate portrait of the extent of his abilities.

Considering that the Bible provides this clarity, why is it that Christians have such divergent views about Satan? Could it be that non-biblical sources of information taint our view of Satan?

Here is the story of one sad chapter in history that reveals how non-biblical views of Satan cast a long, dark shadow over the Christian Church. Perhaps the mistakes of the past can shed some light on this issue in the present.

The witch trials of the sixteenth and seventeenth centuries were accompanied by legendary stories of alleged psychic powers and encounters. European women and men by the tens of thousands were accused of dispensing curses and conjuring demons, and were sentenced to the gallows for hanging or to death by strangulation, followed by burning their lifeless bodies at the flaming stake.

In the midst of the chaos, there were voices of reason. One of those was Reginald Scot, an English justice of the peace who risked his life defending alleged witches. In 1584 at the height of the witch trials, Scot wrote an extensive tome titled *The Discoverie of Witchcraft* that presented devastating arguments against the prevailing view that alleged witches had paranormal powers. He argued both from empirical evidence—exposing some of the tricks used by practitioners of the occult—and from biblical texts to prove that at most those practitioners were tricksters not in possession of truly miraculous powers, and that many others were the innocent victims of mass hysteria fueled by superstition and fear. Scot's points were summarized by Greg Gbur through his webblog, "Skulls in the Stars":

> *"The Discoverie of Witchcraft" itself is a shotgun blast against the belief in witches and the credulous and conniving people who promoted that belief. There are a number of angles from which Scot made his attack:*
>
> - *He argued that belief in witches was inconsistent with a belief in scripture, and even heretical.*

- *He pointed out the flawed and corrupt nature of the witch hunters' investigations, which were clearly designed to justify a guilty verdict.*
- *He presented evidence that mentions of witches in the Bible had been mistranslated and misrepresented.*
- *He highlighted how absurd the claims of witchcraft were and how natural explanations existed for all of them.*
- *He argued that witchcraft had benefited its supposed practitioners so little that, if it were possible, none would bother to make deals with the devil.*
- *He explained how people who believed themselves to be witches were certainly mentally distressed.*
- *He showed how con men and entertainers pretended to do seemingly miraculous tricks by sleight of hand and gave detailed descriptions of these tricks.*[42]

In America, the most notorious witch scare took place in Salem Village, Massachusetts, in 1692. Its death toll—less than 50—paled in comparison to the European toll, but it was no less tragic to those whose lives it devastated. The infamous Salem witch trials began to unfold when a small group of teenage girls within the Puritan community began secretly gathering at the feet of a Barbados slave woman named Tituba. Her wild tales of occult lore fed their imaginations, and soon they began behaving strangely, falling into fits, and accusing people in the community of witchcraft. Their accusation of choice was claiming to be tormented by the "specters" (disembodied spirits) of some of their neighbors.

Imagine that you are one of the accused. One day you hear a knock on your door. You open it to find the town magistrate or his officers informing you that you've been accused of witchcraft and of tormenting several young girls the night before.

"But," you protest, "I was right here in my own house last night. My wife and children can testify to that."

"That may well be," you are told. "But your specter was what tormented the girls. While your physical body was asleep at home, your spiritual body was wandering the neighborhood creating paranormal havoc. The girls claim they saw your specter, and that is enough proof to arrest you."

You're hauled into a damp, rat-infested jail to await trial. It reeks of waste, and you shiver as much from the bitter cold as from the gut-wrenching fear that this may be your last home on Earth. Others just as innocent as you, including one five-year-old child, share the cramped jail cell.

Weeks later, you stand before the authorities in a bizarre kangaroo trial. The afflicted girls sit in the front row. Each time you look at them, they fall into hysterics, collapse on the floor, contort their bodies into grotesque forms, and claim that your specter is tormenting them. You're forced to reach out your hand to touch one of them. When you do, her fits cease, "proving" that you are a witch. You're accused by the girls of heinous crimes and condemned to the gallows. All of your possessions are confiscated. Your family is left with nothing. You're hauled by horse-drawn cart to Gallow's Hill just outside of town, where other fellow "witches" have already met their gruesome fates. A crowd of your neighbors follows.

At the gallows, you stand on top of a ladder leaned against the hanging tree. A noose is placed around your neck. With the crowd watching below, in one desperate final effort to prove your innocence, you recite the Lord's Prayer. After all, it's common knowledge that no witch can say the Lord's Prayer perfectly. But a sincere yet misguided preacher quickly calls out to the crowd that Satan has assumed your shape for a moment, helping you to recite the prayer. The last thing you see in this life are your neighbors standing mute, unwilling—or perhaps unable—to see the absurdity of it all.

The above scenario is a compilation of actual events from various trials and punishments of real people accused during the Salem witch trials. Church and political leaders were swept up in the melee, as was the general populace. Fear of being accused of consorting with the devil turned neighbor against neighbor. Accusations were so commonplace and the penalties so horrific that, just a few weeks into the hysteria, people began to learn how to play the game. The best defense against being accused of witchcraft was a good offense—accusing someone else. Even close-knit families were ripped apart by fear-fueled suspicion. Some sacrificed their own family members to save themselves by testifying against them. Like a firestorm, the fear began feeding on itself, consuming an entire community. Some of Salem's most respected and godly Christians were among the accused. One group of five, as they stood at the gallows, prayed aloud that theirs would be the last innocent blood that was shed and then publicly forgave their accusers.

Once targeted by the girls, you had two choices—maintain your innocence, which only proved that you were guilty, or confess. About fifty of the accused chose to confess rather than face death. Others took a more courageous path and steadfastly maintained their innocence before God and man.

Even today historians debate what caused the girls to react as they did. Some researchers have suggested they were demon-possessed. Others believe the psychotropic nature of ergot, a natural, poisonous fungus found growing on rye, was to blame. An examination of the historical setting of Salem in 1692 confirms there was a great deal of unrest and infighting within the Puritan community at that time, suggesting that some of the accusations may have been politically motivated. But perhaps more than any other single influence is convincing evidence that the girls were both accomplices and victims of the power of suggestion. That's not to say that Satan didn't have a role in the deception and may well have directly influenced at least some of the girls. But the claims of the paranormal that the girls alleged were likely nothing more than the fruits of a powerful social contagion playing on active imaginations.

Tituba was an exotic presence in the austere Puritan community. She held what could arguably be described as an almost hypnotic sway over the girls—not in the sense they were in a trance, but that they responded readily to the slave's bizarre stories with correspondingly peculiar behavior. For these youngsters, whose lives to that point had been socially severe and emotionally sober, the attention they received from the community was an intoxicating brew. It's what psychologists and stage hypnotists call "social proof." The more their behavior was rewarded with attention and affirming feedback, the more "proof" they had that their behavior was accepted by their society. The girls became instant celebrities, with the heady power of life and death over anyone in their path.

Their first accusations were against people in the community who could only be described as easy targets. Sarah Good, a pipe-smoking misfit who begged from house to house, was the first. Given her odd behavior, haggard face, and slovenly attire, it was no great shock to anyone that she might be a witch. She certainly fit the stereotype.

As the girls became bolder, their accusations climbed up the social ladder to more and more esteemed members of the community. Rebecca Nurse, an elderly woman widely respected for her Christian piety and gentle spirit, was targeted. She stood by her innocence throughout the trial, as did a large number of friends and family members who testified to her Christian character. The jury found her innocent. However, when the girls heard the verdict they fell into a rage of convulsions, exclaiming that she was indeed guilty of witchcraft. The magistrates were swayed by their display and asked the jury to reconsider. After reconvening, the jury came back with a guilty verdict. Nurse was hanged. Another of the condemned, George Jacobs, boldly declared before the court, "Well, burn me or hang me, I will stand in the truth of

Christ!" Despite his defiance, or perhaps because of it, they did, in fact, hang him.

"Trial of George Jacobs of Salem for Witchcraft"
by Tompkins Harrison Matteson (1813-1884)

Finally, the girls took aim at one of Massachusetts' wealthiest and most respected citizens, John Alden, the son of John and Pricilla Alden of Mayflower fame. Even *he* was convicted, but escaped jail and went into hiding. But the audacity of the girls was beginning to wear thin for many in the community. A few brave citizens and community leaders took the bold step of questioning the validity of spectral evidence, including Rev. Increase Mather, father of Rev. Cotton Mather, one of the chief witch hunters. Some suggested that the girls were either lying or deluded. Not surprisingly, as the girls' celebrity status gave way to suspicion, their fits began to subside. The girls' fragile house of cards began to quiver in the fresh breeze of truth, and it soon crumbled. Sadly, it was already too late for one hundred and fifty people who were imprisoned and twenty condemned to an appalling death.

Led in part by the clergy, a spiritual cleansing eventually washed over Massachusetts. One of the "tormented" girls, Ann Putnam, stood before her congregation and begged forgiveness for her part in the hysteria. She confessed that she had been deluded by Satan. Some of those who had confessed to being witches recanted, including Tituba. Several jurors who had taken part in the sham trials signed a petition seeking forgiveness from the hundreds of individuals and families they had wronged. The colony observed a day of prayer, fasting, and confession for, as one contemporary called it, "the late Tragedy raised among us by Satan and his Instruments."[43] Like awakening from an all-too-real nightmare, the people of Massachusetts looked back and wondered how they could have been swept into such deception. Fear does strange things to people.

Those of us living in the twenty-first century find it easy to criticize those who perpetrated and fell victim to the deceptions of the witch hysteria. But we can better understand how such deceptions were made possible when we understand the cultural environment in which the hysteria flourished. Suffering, death, privation, and often being constantly surrounded by enemies had a huge impact on the psyches of people of that age. In such environments, the seeds of paranoia and superstition find fertile ground.

The threat of being excommunicated from the church, which was within Puritan culture tantamount to being condemned to Hell for eternity, had to have been a major motivator for extracting confessions. Without a doubt, some of the accused rationalized that it was better to be a forgiven witch than an excommunicated Puritan. An added disadvantage for those who lived over three hundred years ago was a lack of understanding of the frailty of the human mind when faced with deception, especially in the context of gripping fear.

Today we understand more about the power of suggestion over individuals and entire groups than did people long ago. Even so, there have been "witch scares" in sophisticated modern Western culture, such as the Satanic ritual abuse scare of the 1980s and 1990s that put many innocent people in jail, as well as thousands of cases of False Memory Syndrome[44] that have split countless families apart.

The events of 1692 can still speak to us today. Folklore regarding Satan's alleged powers had, over time, crept from the general populous into the Christian Church community. For instance, spectral evidence—the notion that a person's spirit, empowered by demons, could take human form and travel around the community creating havoc— was one of a number of unbiblical folklore superstitions adopted by some in the Puritan church. Despite the obvious discrepancies with Scripture, Satan was afforded powers God had never given him. In this climate, an irrational, unbiblical fear of Satan found a breeding ground for chaos, and in that very real sense, Satan won the day.

Author Nigel Wright, in his book *The Satan Syndrome*, issues this warning to the Church. "The great witch craze gathered momentum because. . . the power and presence of the devil. . . became exaggerated. . . . Such an attitude is not altogether lacking in the contemporary church. . . . When this happens it is scarcely indistinguishable from superstition."[45]

When fear and subjective experience replace God's objective truth, reality is often shoved into the backseat of our minds, leaving the enemy of our souls free to grab the wheel.

Chapter 11
KNOW THINE ENEMY

"Test the spirits to see whether they are from God."
Apostle John, 1 John 4:1

"Superstition ain't the way."
Stevie Wonder

It's amazing how easily psychic powers can be faked and how readily our minds can be deceived. Mentalism is the apparent ability to read minds, predict the future, or influence people's thoughts. I say "apparent" because I want to make it clear that *all* of the mind reading and magic routines in my *Mentallusions* show are tricks. But they are tricks so well disguised that they appear absolutely genuine. Here are just a few of the effects that I present in my show:

- An audience member thinks of a famous actor—someone known only to her—and the celebrity's photo mysteriously appears in an envelope sitting on a chair in full view of the audience the entire show.

- Four men from the audience draw pictures on large pieces of art paper. The papers are then gathered up by another audience member, mixed up, and handed to me. By watching the expressions on the faces of each of the men as I show them the pictures, I'm able to tell who drew which picture.

- Another member of the audience opens a popular novel to any page and merely thinks of any word out of thousands to choose from. In seconds, I reveal her word. Another one chooses a word in the book and, as she visualizes the word, I reveal it one letter at a time merely by touching the tip of her index finger.

Jaws drop. Eyes widen. Someone in the audience exclaims, "Oh my God!" I answer, "No, I think you have me mistaken for someone else. But thanks for the compliment."

On one occasion I was performing for a well-known Christian organization. The audience reaction was, as is typical, very positive. But, a few months later, I was approached by the ministry's director with a concern.

> *"After your program, a group of our volunteers came to me very concerned about the 'psychic' effects you did," the director said. "In fact, they were so concerned that I had to call a special meeting with them. I told them that everything you did was just a trick and that you use those tricks to show how psychic phenomena can be faked. After meeting with them for an hour, try as I might, I could not convince them that what you were doing wasn't the real thing."*

He went on to explain that this group of people had come from a religious and cultural background steeped in occult folklore. Despite the fact that they had since become Christians, they still carried with them the paradigms of the past. Such paradigms—assumptions and values that define the way an individual or community views reality—typically are deeply and emotionally engrained in a person's worldview. In the case of the volunteers, their worldview—although biblical, at least at its core—made room for beliefs not scripturally supportable.

Paradigms are tough nuts to crack and can, when not examined, be barriers to the truth. Even scientists sometimes fall prey to their own paradigms, interpreting data to suit their own worldviews. So, to discover truth in any discipline, each of us, whether Christian or non-Christian, needs to step out of his or her paradigm and examine evidence objectively. That's not to say that all paradigms are wrong, just that they must be examined. For instance, my co-writers and I have spoken to many Christians whose paradigm about Satan included all manner of powers nowhere to be found in the Bible. But upon being confronted with the fact that the Bible presents a very different view of Satan's real powers, they realized that their assumptions had been just that–assumptions–and were certainly not scriptural. Their paradigms then adjusted themselves to accommodate a new set of facts they hadn't been confronted with before. On the other hand, some are comfortable with their paradigms and, despite evidence, choose to remain in their comfort zones.

Paradigms are tough nuts to crack and can, when not examined, be barriers to the truth.

In the past couple of decades, the Spiritual Warfare Movement has become very prevalent in many Christian circles. While the extreme versions do not represent the majority Christian worldview, nearly every denomination has felt its effects. Some prominent proponents of this movement interpret Satan's role in the world as more powerful and pervasive than does Scripture, prescribing specific techniques to thwart Satan's aggressive agenda that are not to be found in the Bible.

To be sure, the Bible tells us in Ephesians Chapter 6 that "we wrestle not against flesh and blood, but against. . . the powers of this dark world and against the spiritual forces of evil in the heavenly realms." Without a doubt, we are at war against Satan, and we must be aware of and responsive to his schemes. He is our enemy. He does have certain powers, particularly powers to deceive. The problem with some proponents of the Spiritual Warfare Movement, including several popular authors, is the *degree* of power they attribute to Satan. In no way do I question the motives or sincerity of most of these teachers. I do, however, have serious reservations about some of their teachings.

One such teaching focuses on "generational curses." This teaching claims that curses can be passed down from generation to generation through the bloodline. The curse can be either brought on by occult practices in the life of an ancestor or a practitioner of the occult placing a curse on that ancestor. If you have the misfortune of having an ancestor in your bloodline with such occult influences, you are—according to many spiritual warfare teachers—in grave jeopardy. One can break these curses, we are told, by repeating formulaic recitations of renunciation that address Satan or his minions directly. The recitations taught in popular spiritual warfare books and seminars are reminiscent of pagan magic rituals. Nowhere in Scripture are we taught the necessity of casting out curses. Rather, we're taught in Galatians 3:13 that "Christ redeemed us from the curse of the law."

The key verse offered by many spiritual warfare teachers to support the notion of generational curses is Exodus 20:5. The verse is in reference to idol worshipers, particularly those who teach their children to worship idols. "You shall not bow down to them or worship them; for I, the Lord your God, am a jealous God, punishing the children for the sin of the fathers to the third and fourth generations of those who hate me."

The clear meaning of the verse, when read in context, is that those who teach their children to hate God bring God's judgment down upon succeeding generations. The curse referred to in the passage is God's curse, not Satan's curse. Reading into this passage the notion that somehow occult curses flow through bloodlines is a stretch, to say the least. In fact, the Bible does not teach that satanic curses pass from generation to generation. The spiritual warfare teaching of generational curses is sadly a case of an occult concept being adapted to Christian teaching.

Other popular spiritual warfare teachings include:

- If you move to a new home or apartment you should cast out evil spirits that may be clinging to the structures and furnishings. I know of one acquaintance who got rid of all of her furniture rather than risk having "possessed" tables, chairs, and couches.
- Staying in a hotel room should be accompanied by a formulaic statement directed at Satan to ward off any evil influences left over by previous occupants. This belief is attuned to pagan animism, the belief in some cultures that spirits inhabit inanimate objects.
- If you have awakened at 3:00 a.m., it could be because Satanists have sent demons out to curse you.
- Children's imaginary friends may be demons. The monsters children fear in their room at night are actually demons.
- Satanists, including some pastors, breed children for sacrifice.
- The medieval belief in evil spirits having sexual relations with humans is real.
- Demons can cause occult practitioners to levitate.
- Occultists under Satan's influence and power can transform themselves into animals and vice versa.
- A popular televangelist teaches that it's a good idea to pray over clothes bought from a second-hand store, in case they have demons attached to them.

If you've not been exposed to these extreme notions being taught in the Christian Church, you may think they are only popular in the far-flung extremes of pseudo-Christian sects. Unfortunately, they are firmly entrenched to varying degrees in many churches of various theological stripes.

Since none of these occult notions are so much as mentioned in the Bible, where do you suppose Christian spiritual warfare teachers and authors find their "evidences" for them? Sadly, each of these teachings has its roots in occult or pagan dogma. Unbelievably, several spiritual warfare authors, in an attempt to bolster their cases, actually quote occult books and practitioners as references. One author who teaches the doctrine of generational curses even acknowledges that the concept is not found in Scripture.

> *Some Christians were born demonized. This is often called by different names, such as generational sin, familial sin, demonic transference, demonic inheritance or the law of the inheritance of evil.* ***Direct and clearly defined biblical teaching or examples of demonic transference are not found in Scripture.***[1] (Emphasis mine)

So to what authoritative source does this author go for his information on generational curses? "Studies in non-Christian religions and occultism reveal this transference to be a fact."[47] One popular spiritual warfare teacher states that "demon cults and the ancestral spirit cults put phenomenal energies into cataloging the demons. They had elaborate ways of finding out the precise name, nature and power of each demon."[48] An author considered by many to be a leading authority on demonology cites as one of his sources a "high ranking occult leader."[49] In another book on spiritual warfare, the author cites a professor at a well-known Christian college who states that his research included gaining inside information from demon contacts who told him the *truth about their lies.*

Let's assume that all of the information cited was from demons or people influenced by Satan. What did Jesus tell us about Satan? "There is no truth in him. When he lies he speaks his native language, for he is a liar and the father of lies" (John 8:44).

Doesn't it seem not only ironic but also downright dangerous to rely on demonically influenced sources as sources of truth? If some key evidences for these teachings are gathered from followers or even former followers of "the father of lies," why in the world would we place *any* trust in those evidences?

The Bible tells us in 1 John 4:1 to "not believe every spirit, but test the spirits to see whether they are from God." The same holds true of teachings regarding spirits. God's Word should be our guiding light when attempting to understand the spirit world, not the dark shadows of occult lore.

Earlier in this book, I mentioned a letter from André Kole about an unexplainable phenomenon he witnessed in Paraguay. In that same correspondence, he affirmed his belief in the supernatural and his assurance of God's sovereignty over our lives, our world, and the forces of darkness in the unseen world.

> *I have had forty continuous years of God's supernatural involvement to continuously bring victory over any negative circumstances. During the past forty years of constantly traveling throughout the world giving thousands of performances. . . the far greatest phenomenon is that I have never missed a performance during those forty years. . . in spite of bomb threats, revolutions, monsoons, earthquakes, and numerous death threats.*
>
> *I remember in Mexico, a signal was to be given by a communist leader for a group in the audience to attack me on stage. They later stated when the signal was given, none of them were able to get up physically from their chairs. It was as if they were glued down.*
>
> *Our tour in India was during the monsoon season, and because of the size of the crowds, most of the meetings were held outside. We would fly into a city and the rains would stop, and then start up again when we left. This went on for seven cities, and we never missed a performance.*
>
> *The point is, so many want to sensationalize events that may or may not have had anything to do with Satan and demons, yet they*

do not sensationalize the far, far greater truth of 'Greater is He who is in us than He who is in the world.' The problem is with the word 'greater' and comprehending how far, far greater God is and the fact that His greatness is infinitely greater to get us through this adventure of life.

People make the whole spiritual warfare so complicated. I stick with one verse that has comforted me through every situation; that is 2 Thessalonians 3:3: "But the Lord is faithful, and he will strengthen you and protect you from the evil one."[50]

Chapter 12
The Deception Within

"Let us not seek our disease out of ourselves; 'tis in us, and planted in our bowels; and the mere fact that we do not perceive ourselves to be sick, renders us more hard to be cured."
Seneca, *Controversiae*, First Century

"We are so constituted that we believe the most incredible things; and, once they are engraved upon the memory, woe to him who would endeavor to erase them."
Goethe, *The Sorrows of Young Werther*, 1774

Diana always had a vivid imagination that transcended her childhood and thrived even into her adulthood. "Vivid" actually might not be the right word. Diana's fantasies featured her as the heroine in wildly vibrant adventures that seemed almost as real as her "normal" life.

"I always thought about things that tended to be out of the normal experiences," she remembers. "They didn't feel like they were the usual little daydreams. They were different—more real."[51]

Spiritual warfare was of particular interest to Diana as an adult. As she delved into books and attended seminars on the topic, she became convinced that satanic conspiracies lurked beneath all manner of high-level global events. Then, one day a childhood friend called to confess to her that as children she and Diana had witnessed satanic ritual murders perpetrated by none other than Diana's father—memories long repressed because of the horrific trauma they both experienced. After meeting with a Christian therapist who specialized in regression and recovered memories, Diana's apparent emerging memories of the crimes took on more detail. "It seemed so detailed, so real," she later recalled. "It was like watching a movie."[52]

Regression Therapy and False Memory Syndrome

Diana checked herself into an inpatient program for victims of satanic ritual abuse. In that reinforcing environment, members of the group sessions and her therapist encouraged her to dredge up ghastly details including when Diana herself lifted a huge boulder and crushed a man's skull. With the assistance of group therapy, the detailed memories began to gush forth like a tsunami, then sucked her deeper into a whirlpool of depression and suspicion. If anyone dared to question the reality of the recovered memories or suggest they were manufactured fantasies, they were accused of hurting everyone else in the group. Every image that came to mind, she was assured, must be true.

Diana eventually cooperated with police, who had been investigating murders alleged by her childhood friends. Her parents and five other families were served with warrants. Backhoes dug up their yards searching for evidence. But none was found, even after months of investigation. The women's stories began to unravel. Diana's allegations and the ensuing "hell on Earth" devastated her parents, who could not understand what had happened to their daughter to cause her to make up such wildly fantastic and damning accusations.

Then Diana came across an article on false memory syndrome, and a glimmer of doubt cracked through the bleak darkness of memories she had sworn were real. Eventually, she met with a former regression therapist named Dr. Paul Simpson, who explained to her how the mind can, under certain circumstances and with the help of regression therapy, create "memories" of things that never took place. People with very vivid imaginations, especially those open to suggestion, are particularly susceptible to therapies often used to recover "lost memories." She realized too late that she had been the victim, not of Satanic ritual abuse, but of another kind of abuse—a pseudo-therapy that preyed on the vulnerable.

Diana took the bold step to contact her parents—from whom she had cut off all contact—in an attempt to reconcile. Her parents did forgive her and reconciliation took place, but Diana says, "There will always be scars. It will never be like this never happened." [53]

Simpson is widely regarded as one of the world's leading experts on recovered memories—the apparent ability of some people to recover long-lost memories of horrific abuse often committed by family members or trusted friends. Under the guidance of a therapist trained in recovered memory therapy, these victims are allegedly able to dredge from deep within their subconscious detailed memories they had buried years prior.

To bring these memories to the surface, therapists often employ what is known as regression therapy, during which the patient is hypnotically guided back to his or her past. Once "inside" the past, patients discover long-forgotten details of abuse. Quite often the perpetrators of the abuses are part of a deeply secretive, satanic cult. According to Simpson, thousands of people, often family members, have been accused, and many convicted, of heinous crimes, facing imprisonment.[54]

Once a proponent and practitioner of recovered memory therapy, Simpson discovered years into his career that the human mind is capable of more deception than even he, a highly trained psychologist, had ever suspected. He discovered that he and other therapists who used regression therapy were, in fact, helping their clients create false memories while they were in a highly suggestible state brought on by the therapists themselves. Incidentally, regression therapy is the same technique used to regress clients who recover memories of past lives and even alien abductions.

It's undeniable that many people have been abused by trusted family members and friends. But memories of actual abusive events, according to Simpson, tend to be remembered, not repressed. Details of memories will, over time, deteriorate to an extent, but the gist of a traumatic memory will, for the most part, stay intact.[55]

Simpson became one of the strongest critics of recovered memory therapy, and, in time, several high profile lawsuits greatly reduced the practice of recovered therapy among licensed therapists. However, some unlicensed counselors still use the technique including, sadly enough, some in Christian counseling settings. The technique used by some Christian counselors is very similar to regression therapy, in which the client is encouraged to regress to his or her past with the Holy Spirit as the guide. It is sometimes called "prayer visualization" or "Holy Spirit guidance," described here by Simpson:

> *First they have the client close her eyes, and then empty herself of any distracting thoughts or images. The regressionist then prays that the 'Holy Spirit' will come upon the person and take her back in time to unlock forgotten traumas. . . . This is a description of hypnosis, plain and simple. It involves the same standard induction steps that allow a person to move into a relaxed state of trance.*[56]

How have Christian counselors—who claim to use the Bible as their central guiding source of truth—become so enamored by a technique that would lead them and their clients into such deception? Simpson points out that misguided professionals, including him, lost their way when they accepted a view of the "Holy Spirit as guide to repressed memories" that is biblically unsupportable:

> *Historically the Christian community has always pressed forward to a higher standard in our search for truth. For us the bottom line for any belief or practice is, 'Is this in harmony with the Word of God?' Amazingly, we have abandoned this standard when it comes to the subject of regression therapies. This much we know for sure, regressionism is not a doctrine taught anywhere in the Bible.*[57]

Nowhere in any of Christ's teachings is recovery of forgotten memories implied or taught. It is only as we come to embrace Christ and His teachings, His truth, that we come to know true freedom. So whose "truth" are regressionists referring to? Regressionism, a Freudian belief system, emphasizes that its disciples must live with a backward focus, spending years and vast amounts of time and money in search of hidden incest, prior lives, or space alien memories that are suspected to have occurred decades or centuries ago. Once these hypnotic images are experienced, the client gives them center stage in her life, is never allowed to question their reality, and descends into an ever darker stairway of rage, bitterness, selfishness, hate, and isolation. Simpson continues:

> *In sharp contrast, Scripture teaches a forward-looking focus. 'But one thing I do: Forgetting what is behind and straining toward what is ahead, I press on toward the goal to win the prize for which God has called me heavenward in Christ Jesus.' (Philippians 3:13-14) As we live out Christ's truth, we naturally bear fruit of 'love, joy, peace, forbearance, kindness, goodness, faithfulness, gentleness and self-control. . . .' (Galatians 5:22-23). Believers learn to value others as greater than themselves and their lives reflect service and sacrifice. Paul challenges us, 'Do not conform any longer to the pattern of this world, but be transformed by the renewing of your mind. Then you will be able to test and approve what God's will is—his good, pleasing and perfect will' (Romans 12:2 NIV). Regression disciples allow themselves to become enslaved to their own horrific thoughts, engrossed in each sordid detail. But Christ's teachings and truth are diametrically opposed to these beliefs and practices.*[58]

So, how is it that some people are drawn to fantastic flights of imagination and find it difficult to distinguish between them and reality? Part of the answer lies in the strange and fascinating world of what researchers call "fantasy-prone personalities" and "Grade 5 Syndrome."

Fantasy-prone Personalites

Fantasy-prone people have an amazing ability to fantasize in vivid detail. Many describe these experiences as "real as real." Generally speaking, they are not psychotic and are, in fact, high functioning normal people holding down successful careers and long-standing marriages and relationships. You wouldn't know that they often spend a significant portion of their days fantasizing another "reality," because they've become very adept at being secretive about their intense fantasies. At times their fantasies are involuntary, triggered by a person or object around them. In some cases, they can hear, smell, visualize, and feel their fantasies. Most confuse their fantasies with reality.

Simpson makes a revealing point regarding the connection between fantasy-prone personalities and claims of alien encounters, saying that one study showed that people who claim to have been abducted by space alients are not pathological but fit the profile for fantasy-prone personality.[59] Psychologists Sheryl C. Wilson and Theodore X. Barber published ground-breaking research in the 1980s, estimating that about four percent of the population is fantasy-prone. If that's accurate, that would be over 12 million people in the United States alone.

Their research revealed that fantasy-prone people typically exhibit some or many of these characteristics:

- Being excellent hypnotic subjects
- Having imaginary friends in childhood and fantasizing often as child

- Having an actual fantasy identity
- Experiencing imagined sensations as real
- Having vivid sensory perceptions
- Having reputed paranormal and mystical experiences (i.e., claiming psychic powers, encountering apparitions, reliving past experiences, having out-of-body experiences, communicating with higher Intelligences or spirits, claiming to be abducted by aliens)
- Believing they have powers for spiritual healing or faith healing
- Having hypnagogic hallucinations (waking dreams)[60]

Dr. Simpson summarized how individuals with fantasy-prone personalities genuinely experience hypnotic phenomena:

> *The data show hypnotic phenomena are natural for some individuals. Fantasy-prone personalities have many experiences throughout their lives that are similar to the classical hypnosis experiences, and they find the suggestions of the hypnotist are very harmonious with their own ongoing experiential life. . . . There are individuals who have a lifetime history of intense fantasy, who have developed hallucinatory abilities, and who—as a result of these talents—are able to quickly, easily, and profoundly experience the classic hypnotic phenomena.*[61]

Simpson's work and the Wilson-Barber study explain how those phenomena may mimic psychic or supernatural events for the subjects, but are actually hallucinatory fantasy.

Stage hypnotists rely on a psychosocial phenomenon called "social contagion" to affect bizarre and often hilarious responses from their subjects. If you've ever witnessed a stage hypnosis show, you've no doubt noticed that once the hypnotist has placed the subjects into a heightened state of relaxation and suggestibility (called a hypnotic induction), he then encourages the crowd to applaud the subjects when they follow the hypnotist's instructions. He will also reinforce the desired behavior of the subjects to encourage them to continue following his instructions.

When used in a stage hypnosis show, it can be very entertaining and harmless. But social contagion in less innocuous situations can also trigger some people to behave in socially unacceptable and even harmful ways. Two examples of social contagion are when riots break out in large crowds or rabid sports fans get out of hand after a game. The reinforcement from others joining in the melee begins to spiral out of control and can end in tragedy. Although technically not hypnosis, a form of social contagion is at work feeding the mob mentality.

Sadly, there are also examples from the Christian world. One popular televangelist is known for waving his jacket wildly in the direction of a section of the adoring crowd, resulting in scores of pre-conditioned audience members falling over like bowling pins. The claim is that the televangelist releases "Holy Ghost power" when, in fact, the highly suggestible crowd is responding to social contagion.

The girls involved in the Salem witch trial accusations were likely not only fantasy-prone, but susceptible to the social contagion in the community which reinforced their bizarre behavior. Many, if not most, of those who have implicated family members as an outcome of recovered memory therapy were not only fantasy-prone, but the reinforcement they received from regression therapists and in group therapy while they were in highly suggestible states reinforced their fantasy-prone-induced "memories."

Grade 5 Syndrome

Hypnosis researchers often use a 1-5 scale called the Hypnotic Induction Profile to measure the hypnotizability of those they are researching. Those in the 4 and 5 categories are considered highly hypnotizable. Hypnosis researcher Herbert Spiegel's work revealed that between five to ten percent of the population are what he termed "hypnotic virtuosos" and are categorized as having Grade Five Syndrome. Like fantasy-prone personalities, these people are generally high functioning but have an astonishing capacity to fantasize. Grade Fives can spontaneously place themselves into a highly suggestible state with or without the help of a hypnotist.

Investigative reporter and senior editor of *Cornerstone Magazine*, Jon Trott, in his review of Grade Five Syndrome wrote:

> *Grade Fives are particularly vulnerable to something Spiegel calls 'the compulsive triad.' The first point of the triad, compulsive compliance, is a fancy way of saying that, in a trance state, fives feel an all-but-overwhelming urge to comply with someone suggesting a new or variant viewpoint. The second leg of the triad, source amnesia, means basically that the Grade Five who comes up with certain information is unable to recall where the information actually came from. The third element, rationalization, occurs when the Grade Five encounters logical opposition to his or her adopted viewpoint.*[62]

Simpson describes the common thread woven into the fabric of many extraordinary but evidence-lacking claims when he says that "fantasy-prones and Grade Fives provide the strongest clues for how healthy people can be pulled into a delusional world of horrific fantasies."[63]

There is a vital lesson handed down to today's Christian Church by the victims of Salem, the extremes of the Spiritual Warfare Movement, and the tragedies resulting from false memory syndrome. Although the majority of us may not fall into those depths of deception, we can, in perhaps more subtle ways, stumble over unfounded assumptions, including assigning to Satan more power than he holds over us, or that we are more immune to deceit than we actually are.

Too often, Christians feel more invulnerable to deceit than we should be, because we have biblical truth on our side.

That well-placed confidence in God's Word can, however, turn to pride and a lack of discernment when we don't combine that confidence in Him with a humble awareness that *we can* be deceived.

Proverbs 16:18 warns, "Pride goes before destruction, a haughty spirit before a fall." Jeremiah 17: 9 adds, "The heart is deceitful above all things and beyond cure. Who can understand it?" Each of us, Christian or non-Christian, is in possession of a heart that is deceitful at its core. We *can* be fooled and tend to stumble down the path to deceit when left to our own understanding. That's why God tells us in Proverbs 3:5-6: "Trust in the *LORD* with *all your heart* and lean *not* on your *own* understanding; in *all* your ways submit to him, and he *will* make *your* paths straight." (Emphasis mine.)

How do we avoid reliance on our own understanding, which so often leads to deceit, and find the straight path to truth? Psalm 119:105 provides the simple but profound answer: "Your word is a lamp for my feet, a light on my path."

Chapter 13

POWER AND FEAR: DECEPTION'S FUEL

"The most difficult person to deceive is the one who loves the truth more than they fear their pain."
Dan Korem

"Here is the world. Beautiful and terrible things will happen. Don't be afraid."
Frederick Buechner

James Hydrick was a miracle man to millions of people in the early 1980s. A young martial arts instructor who performed feats like knocking a man off of his feet with a punch only one inch away and push-ups using only his thumb as support, his physical skills were impressive. But what catapulted him into national stardom were the psychic skills he claimed were developed by studying under a Chinese martial arts master.

A dollar bill perched on the tip of a nail and covered by an inverted fish tank rotated at his command. Pencils rotated and pages of a phone book flipped over without any threads, magnets, or other gimmicks—using just his penetrating gaze and the wave of his hand. His charismatic personality, charming boyish good looks, and apparent sincerity made his impressive feats all the more believable.

In an Associated Press story, news writer Verne Anderson was certainly impressed.

> *James Hydrick moves pencils by pointing at them, catches deer with his bare hands and blocks punches and finds objects while blindfolded. . . .*
>
> *But there's more to the gentle 21-year-old ex-con than a bag of eye-popping parlor tricks. His mind-over-matter skills are indeed amazing, but his odyssey from discarded infant to master of martial arts is downright bizarre. . . .*
>
> *Hydrick arrived in Salt Lake City last summer to set up a martial arts school based on his knowledge of Wushu Gung Fu, an ancient Chinese discipline aimed at achieving complete mental and physical self-control. . . .*
>
> *Hydrick has, at various times and always in the presence of reporters, done the following:*
>
> - *Turned pages of telephone books from ten feet away and moved pens, pencils, and plants and other objects by giving them hard stares.*
> - *Blocked punches and found hidden coins or car keys while blindfolded.*
> - *Walked blindfolded down a line of sixteen people and, without touching them, knew which were men and which were women.*
> - *Sneaked up on deer at night and grabbed them around the neck.*
> - *Demonstrated a level of martial arts judged by experts to be expert.*
>
> *'Hydrick is eager to pass on his peculiar skills to others. Already a six-year-old pupil can move pencils and plants,' Anderson said.*
>
> *'I intend to have a monastery, a temple, and train people the way of life,' Hydrick said.'* [64]

James Hydrick was, indeed, well on his way to becoming a religious leader or, perhaps more to the point, the founder of a new cult.

About this time, Dan Korem received a call from a seminary student friend named Rob Martin. Martin's brother was a devotee of Hydrick's and had recently experienced an emotional breakdown, triggered by his association with Hydrick. Martin was deeply concerned that his brother had fallen under demonic influence by the satanically empowered, miracle-working Hydrick.

Korem had already read the article about Hydrick and, as a seasoned illusionist, was convinced that Hydrick was using clever tricks to convince both his followers and the millions who watched him on nationwide television that he had paranormal powers. Korem attempted to convince Martin that his brother had fallen for a lie rather than any kind of true powers, but Martin was not convinced.

That phone call set into motion a months-long investigation of Hydrick's alleged powers, during which Korem posed as a producer of a television program featuring the young psychic. During the production, Korem duplicated Hydrick's feats, much to the psychic's shock. Eventually, Hydrick admitted on camera that he was, in fact, using tricks. The resulting production became the first nationwide television special during which a person claiming to have psychic powers confessed that they were a fraud.

In the documentary, which was later nominated for a Pulitzer Prize, James Hydrick's past came to light, revealing that he had been severely abused and molested as a child, which Korem states fueled his drive to deceive:

> *The devastation of Hydrick's family and subsequent abuse chiseled out a mindset that believed 'love is a trick,' and spun him into a fantasy world where another human need—recognition—became a perverted pursuit. With a clever mind, he found recognition by feeding off of a cultural desire to have and believe in one's own personal powers: "Because a lot of adults are looking for something like this. They want to believe that something like this exists."*[65]

Asked why he perpetuated the lie, Hydrick confessed, "My whole idea behind this in the first place was to see how dumb America was. How dumb the world is."[66]

Following the airing of "Psychic Confession," the U.S. Department of Health and Human Services purchased the documentary to educate social workers on the effects of child abuse. Today, Korem consults with law enforcement agencies, corporations, and government agencies, including NASA, instructing them on effective personality profiling. Although Hydrick ultimately thanked Korem for exposing him, there is a sad footnote to his story. The former fraudulent psychic was sentenced to seventeen years in prison in 1989 for molesting five young boys. He was then remanded to a psychiatric hospital where, at last report, he remains.

I've had the privilege of meeting with Korem on a couple of occasions. I asked him during one meeting in Dallas what type of personality is most vulnerable to deception. Though Dan did not single out a "most vulnerable" personality type, he did offer a very insightful response: "The most difficult person to deceive is the one who loves the truth more than they fear their pain."

Conversely, someone who fears their pain more than they love the truth is wide open to deceit. That seminal statement by Korem offers a key to why so many people fall for the claims of psychics and deceptions of all kinds. Fear can be a profoundly negative force in all of our lives. We will often go to extremes to avoid or rid ourselves of it. Unless one is firmly planted in a love for truth, fear can take over and lead to destruction.

Consider the case of French clairvoyant Maria Duval, whose organization has duped millions of the most vulnerable people around the world—the elderly, poor, and sick—into sending her and her cohorts hundreds of millions of dollars in exchange for cheap trinkets with supposed psychic powers to ward off their bad fortune, to rid them of their pain.

Investigators have called it one of the most notorious mail fraud cases in history. The organization hired mailing houses to send letters to mostly elderly people whose information was purchased from data brokers. These lists are known as "sucker lists" in the direct mail industry. Letters by the millions were then sent ostensibly from Duval promising good fortune if enough money was sent to the famous psychic.

Unless one is firmly planted in a love for truth, fear can take over and lead to destruction.

In early 2016, *CNN Money* launched an investigation into the Duval syndicate and discovered a maze of deeply-concealed companies and individuals operating the massive fraud. As much as $500,000 in checks were processed every two weeks by the mailing firm hired by the fraudulent organization. The mailing firm would, in the process, throw away personal mementos such as hair and photos, sent to Duval at her request by her devotees. Although it is unknown how many people worldwide have been taken in, the U.S. Postal Service estimates that over 1.4 million people in the United States alone have been victims.

Here are just a few of the comments from desperate people held in the snare of the Duval mystique as reported by *CNN Money*. Most fell into the trap and were then manipulated because of fear for their health, finances, or relationships:

- A military veteran sent Duval four thousand dollars in hopes that she would bless his lottery numbers so he could afford to live in an assisted living home.
- A woman duped by the psychic reported, "All she wanted from me is money. Now I am homeless and five thousand dollars in debt. I need dental care, and I have no money to pay."
- A seventeen-year-old U.K. girl was found dead in a river in 1998 with a letter from Duval in her pocket. Her mother told the paper that her daughter had been corresponding with Duval for weeks before her death. "Clare used to be

a happy girl but she went downhill after getting involved with all this," her mother said.

- "She [Duval] was eagerly waiting on my disability check," complained another victim.

In some cases, the Duval letters took a more sinister tone—suggesting that misfortune awaited those who ignored her. *CNN Money* reported, "In 1997, one woman told the Scottish *Daily Record & Sunday Mail* newspaper that she was terrified of what would happen if she didn't send money. 'When I wrote to say I didn't have that kind of cash, the letters got even more frightening,' she said at the time. 'I was so scared I couldn't eat or sleep worrying whether I'd be hit by more bad luck. I was convinced I'd need further heart surgery and this time I might not survive.'"[67]

The most difficult person to deceive is the one who loves the truth more than they fear their pain.

Both the Duval organization's victims and those of countless other psychic scammers number in the many millions, but most have one thing in common—a desperate fear that drives them to embrace deceit. Deceit's casualties aren't only those taken in by psychic scams. We are all susceptible to its deceptive charms, regardless of the disguise it wears. For you and me, it may be some other form of deception that marshals the power of fear in our lives, leading us toward promises that seem enticing but escort us into an ambush.

Korem's sage advice about loving the truth more than fearing our pain is foundational to leading lives less vulnerable to deception. What truths should we embrace to help inoculate us from deceit? Here's one that millions through the centuries have found invaluable: "For God has not given us the spirit of fear; but of power, love, and a sound mind." (2 Timothy 1:7)

Section Two

Unmasking the Fear

Toby A. Travis, Ed.D.

Earlier in this book we discovered scriptural and empirical evidence that much of what has been assumed to be demonic or otherwise unearthly paranormal powers are, in fact, more deception than reality. This second of three sections focuses on Satan's powers as defined through the Bible. Should Satan be feared and, if so, under what circumstances is that fear appropriate? In 2003, *The Global Journal of Classic Theology* published an essay by former illusionist and Christian educator Dr. Toby A. Travis entitled "Whom Shall We Fear?" that presents a timeless message about the limits of Satan's powers and how unwarranted fear of our enemy often limits our effectiveness as Christians.

Dr. Travis' perspective as both a world-class illusionist, a seasoned scholar, and leader in education offers us a unique opportunity to dive more deeply into this topic and emerge with a greater understanding of both deception and fear. With his permission, we are very happy to include excerpts of his classic and important essay in this book. In addition, he has added several personal stories of encounters with paranormalists, along with some important updates for this publication.

Dr. Toby A. Travis: Photo by Juan Manuel Pastor

About Toby A. Travis

Dr. Toby A. Travis is an educator, researcher, trainer, speaker, consultant, and author. He officially retired from performing as an illusionist and as a theatrical producer in 2008. Since that time, he has served as a school administrator and as a consultant and trainer, assisting private and independent schools in the areas of strategic planning, leadership, and academic development.

Dr. Travis earned his Doctorate in Education through Louisiana Baptist University, specializing in Christian School Administration. His dissertation is entitled "The Trusted School Leader: Gaining Better Results, Deeper Stakeholder Relationships, and Greater Stability."

From an early age Toby was captivated by the art of illusion and studied under some of the most gifted magicians in the industry, including Robert Thrasher and André Kole. Travis toured the world as a celebrated illusionist for over twenty years, producing one of the largest full-scale touring illusion shows in the United States as well as touring with his solo performances throughout the US, UK, Europe, Central America, South America, and South Asia.

As an illusionist and theatrical producer, Travis has received numerous awards and recognitions by the Society of American Magicians, the International Brotherhood of Magicians, The Magic Circle (London), el Círculo Mágico (Ecuador), the Sri Lanka Magic Circle, and the Fellowship of Christian Magicians (USA and UK).

His published works include: "The Professional Amateur: A Handbook for Variety Artists," "Searching the Supernatural," "Maximum Impact Strategies," "Paranormal Lies & Wonders," and "KnowFooling."

(Learn more about Toby Travis at: www.trustedschoolleader.com.)

Chapter 14

WHOM SHALL WE FEAR?

"The oldest and strongest emotion of mankind is fear,
and the oldest and strongest kind of fear is fear of the unknown."
H. P. Lovecraft

As a young teenager, I had the privilege of becoming the protégé of the gifted and talented entertainer and magician, Robert Thrasher. He had recently retired when I first met him, and without asking for any type of remuneration, Bob poured his time, skills, and energy into this young and eager thespian and helped me to launch a career as a performer before I was old enough to drive a car. By the time I was fifteen, I was acting, singing, and performing as a magician for clubs and schools and private parties—and people were actually paying me to do it! Bob saw "magic" as just a great hobby and a part-time job. He never had any grand plans for me to become an illusionist and inspirational speaker touring the world; all of that happened years later.

When I was twenty, I was challenged by some Christian friends to begin using my skills in the art of illusion in conjunction with ministry. At first, the idea didn't seem to make sense to me. Could I really put "magic" and "ministry" together? But after being introduced to and inspired by evangelist and illusionist André

Kole, I put together my first ministry event utilizing "magic," the art of illusion.

For over twenty years I toured as an illusionist, assisting hundreds of churches and para-church organizations around the world in creatively reaching their communities with the Gospel of Jesus Christ.[68] Through the use of these creative outreach events, we were able to reach tens of thousands who were not being reached through more traditional means of evangelism and outreach.

Promotional photo from the "Illusion & Beyond" tour featuring Toby Travis (2000)

Not long after I began using "magic" in ministry, I also began to receive numerous calls, notes, and letters from Christians who were confused about what I was doing and wondering how my "magic" differed from what they believed Satan and his demons were able to do. They were good questions—ones that motivated me to study the Bible more closely and to discover why people could be confused between the art of illusion and supposed occult powers.

I was so motivated, in fact, that I went on to complete a bachelor's degree in theology and a master's degree in religious education. While pursuing those degrees, I took the opportunity to apply my studies to this topic, and it is my hope that what I discovered will serve as a resource to you in bringing clarity to an often very confusing subject.

Many Christians have developed their beliefs about the occult and presumed satanic powers not from a study of Scripture, but rather through the influence movies, fictional books, TV shows, tabloid journalism, television and radio preachers, as well as stories based on personal accounts rather than facts or research. It seems that we are bombarded daily with images and messages that support claims of amazing and powerful occult and demonic activity. But are these claims true? To what extent do Christians critically apply a biblical analysis to these sources of information? Do the biblical records reinforce these claims, or do they provide a strikingly different portrayal of satanic and occult powers than what we see portrayed in the media and coming from the majority of popular media outlets, or what we hear from many evangelical Christian teachers and preachers?

Have you ever wondered why it is that many Christians who say they have "victory in Christ" and proclaim that "Satan is a defeated foe" live in fear of Satan's attacks and demonic oppression? A study of the Bible demonstrates that fear (defined both as "terror" and as "awe") is an attribute of worship that should be reserved for our relationship to God and no one else. For example, Deuteronomy 6:13 says, "You shall fear only the Lord your God." In addition, when Jesus described Satan as the "father of lies" in John 8:44, what did He mean? What are Satan's powers in the "end times," and why does Paul in 2 Thessalonians 2:9 describe Satan's activity during those days as "counterfeit" or "imitation miracles?"

Let's look at a biblical worldview of the nature, character, and activity of the one whom so many fear, and discover the answer to these questions and the key query, "Whom Shall We Fear?"

Chapter 15

Living in the Illudere

"One sometimes weeps over one's illusions with as much bitterness as over a death."

Guy de Maupassant

The word "illusion" originates from the Latin, *illudere*, which means "an erroneous perception of reality"—to see reality incorrectly. As an illusionist and a student of biblical Christianity, I am part of a group of professionals who have been sought out by many individuals over the years to help them discern if they are living in the *illudere*. As we have interviewed, counseled, and simply conversed with these individuals, we have encountered many who are living in the *illudere* concerning the supernatural. In particular, they are seeing reality incorrectly when it comes to claims of the paranormal.

Foundational to what may be an erroneous (non-biblical) view of the spiritual world—particularly as it relates to the paranormal—is fear of the Occult, of satanic images, of demonic objects, and of personal attacks and influence of the paranormal. However, by gaining a clear understanding of what the biblical writers have to say about Satan's true powers and limitations, they can experience freedom from the fears that are often part of living in the *illudere*.

For many, study of the claims of the paranormal from the New Age movement, Eastern mysticism, and the Occult is a scary venture. To be sure, exploring such practices out of mere curiosity and without biblical discernment can be emotionally and spiritually dangerous. However, to approach these claims fearfully is to play into the hands of those who are making such claims. It may be that the strength or power of paranormal proponents and claimants is primarily in their ability to generate fear and an unholy awe.

As Christians, the Bible instructs us over and over again to "fear God and God only."[69] Apart from the fear of God, we are to live without fear, for "greater is He that is in us than He that is in the world."[70] To accept the claims of paranormal practitioners without challenging them is to offer them a level of credibility that according to Jesus they simply do not possess.[71] At its core, Satan's rebellion was caused by the desire to be God. Thus, his desire is for us to fear him as a god and to fear his destructive activity.

There is little doubt that the first century Christians believed in a very real spiritual world and that they also attributed supernatural magical powers to evil spirits. In the opening chapter of his fine work on this subject, *Powers of Darkness*, Clinton Arnold makes the following statement:

> *In Western culture we have come to think of magic as harmless trickery in the context of entertainment. When we speak of magic during the period of the New Testament, however, we must realize it was not the art of illusion. Magic represented a method of manipulating good and evil spirits to lend help or bring harm. Magical formulas could be used for such things as attracting a lover or winning a chariot race. Black magic, or sorcery, involved summoning spirits to accomplish all kinds of evil deeds. Curses could be placed, competitors subdued, and enemies restrained.*[72]

We should be quick to agree with Arnold that the activity of evil spirits should never be considered "harmless trickery." However, the appearance of "magical formulas manipulating good and evil spirits to lend help. . . bring harm. . . attract lovers. . . win chariot races. . ." may in fact *have been* an illusion. Again, it is nearly certain that citizens of the first century believed these powers to be genuine, but were they? Was too much credit given to the extraordinary powers and claims of evil spirits and of Satan himself? Noted lawyer, professor, and theologian John Warwick Montgomery is a prolific author and "considered by many as the foremost living apologist for biblical Christianity."[73] Montgomery provides a keen example of how easy it is for the spiritually minded person to attribute to Satan more than he should.

> *The pietist is tricked by Satan's lie to Jesus when he tempted our Lord in the wilderness (Luke 4:5-6). In point of fact, the kingdoms of the world were not Satan's to give. They remained entirely in God's hands, and were thus Christ's already. . . . The pietist takes Satan too seriously when he claims to control the world; he should recognize, as the book of Job so clearly teaches, that the Evil One operates on a stringently controlled scale, within the strict framework of God's sovereign will.*[74]

The "pietist" was living in the *illudere,* and like today's popular culture within and outside of the evangelical Christian Church, many are quick to glorify the activity of Satan and attribute to him powers and authorities that he does not possess.

Palatable Lies

Why are we instructed in the Bible to "fear God alone?" The answer is in understanding that fear is an element of worship. When fear is present, there is also a sense or state of awe.

Consider the success and popularity of the many books written which glorify and exhibit the claimed powers of "the dark side." In recent decades, books about Satan's miraculous intervention in human affairs have sold millions of copies in the Christian marketplace.

For years, a talented comedian toured the United States as a popular Christian speaker whose initial success (and the attention given to him from the evangelical Christian community) was due largely to the popularity of his book, *The Satan Seller,* which featured a vivid testimony of witnessing the miraculous powers of Satan. Although it may not have been the author's purpose, his presentations fostered and fueled a fear of Satan and his activities in the world. The limelight was no longer on the comedian; in 1992 his book and supposed satanic involvement were exposed as fabrications.[75] The Satanists' tales that he presented were just that—fictitious stories created to tickle the ears of those who were enamored by the fear of claimed satanic powers.

The Evil One operates on a stringently controlled scale, within the strict framework of God's sovereign will.

The irony of it all is that Christians, who should be the most discerning when examining truth claims, have fallen for the lies perpetuated by both the occult world and, tragically, other Christians. This lack of discernment on the part of believers in Christ only plays into Satan's hands. If paranormal proponents can keep an air of mystery and darkness about them, they will continue to maintain their images of transcendent knowledge and dark miraculous powers. These proponents make such claims as, "A ten-thousand-year-old guru speaks through me," or "I predict that there will be a major earthquake in California this month," or "I can psychically alter your energies and restore your health." It is alarming that many within the Christian Church do not question the honesty of these claims. Christians, in fact, may be largely responsible for the spread of misinformation and unfounded truth claims, due to their predisposition to believe in the supernatural and desire for spiritual experiences.

For a large portion of evangelical Christians, claims of paranormalists go unquestioned. According to one study by Erich Goode, there is a strong link between holding to a Christian worldview and to the claims of the paranormal. "As a general rule, persons who accept articles of traditional, fundamentalist Christian faith. . . tend also to accept a range of paranormal beliefs as well."[76] This sometimes unquestioning acceptance of what supporters of the paranormal teach as truth may be due to an uncritical acceptance of the media's portrayal of the occult and a faulty understanding of Satan's role in our world. This has created a wicked brew of palatable lies.

Chapter 16

UNMASKING SATAN'S POWERS

"Pay no attention to the man behind the curtain!"
L. Frank Baum, *The Wonderful Wizard of Oz*

A few years back I was invited to be a keynote speaker at a conference dedicated to helping attendees see the world and events in their own lives through a Biblical perspective. Over the course of an hour and a half, I talked about how to identify the unique powers of God. I walked my audience through nearly all of the references found in the Old and New Testaments, which repeatedly remind readers that only God possesses the attributes of omniscience (that God alone has all knowledge), omnipresence (that all of creation is in the presence of God), and omnipotence (that only God has power over all creation). I specifically drew a parallel between God's unique powers and belief in the paranormal.

Following the seminar, I was standing in front of the auditorium, leaning back against the stage, taking some clarifying questions from six or seven individuals who were trying to reconcile their personal experiences with what they had just learned about a Christian worldview of the paranormal. One gentleman was quite upset with what he had heard and seemed intent on challenging me.

After I had clarified a couple of questions from others, he loudly stated for the entire hall to hear, "I heard everything you had to say tonight sir, but you don't know my neighbor. She's a witch!" Instantly, all eyes were on him—even those who were starting to leave the auditorium turned around to listen to his claim.

I said, "Really? How do you know?"

His response appeared to be a practiced narrative, as he began to regale a rather dramatic and engaging story of his neighbor lady, "the witch". It was fascinating to watch those around him. With every suspenseful detail shared, his audience grew in number. Our "after-session" conversation had started with a small group of just a half-dozen, but within minutes he had attracted a group of forty to fifty individuals who found their way down to the front of the hall, gathering closely around us and hanging on his every word.

The story he told was compelling and amazing. He disclosed how he was an eye-witness to his neighbor being able to accurately predict the future, to cause a wound from a serious cut to heal, and to command a candle to levitate and float across the room. As he told his tale, it was obvious that others were quick to acknowledge and accept his story as legitimate, as I saw their eyes intensely fixed upon him and their faces showing expressions of amazement. As he went on and on, it occurred to me exactly why Steven King makes such a good living. People love a scary story.

But then, I interrupted.

I said, "Excuse me. But I'm fascinated with your story. If your neighbor lady, the witch, truly possesses these divine attributes, it would certainly be strong evidence to the contrary of a Christian worldview."

He responded, "Exactly. That's my point!" And he grinned.

"So," I said, "I would love to meet her." It was only about 8 pm in the evening. "May I follow you home now, and would you please introduce me to her?"

Instantly his demeanor changed, his countenance lowered, and he began to mumble.

"Well, well, she… she's not my neighbor anymore."

People love a scary story.

"Where does she live now?" I asked. And at that he began to step back and move away from me into the center aisle of the auditorium, bumping into a few of his audience members.

"Well," he mumbled, as he continued to back further away from me, "she lives in another city now."

I stepped toward him and asked, "Where is that exactly?"

Visibly annoyed, he barked back at me while walking backwards, trying to create a greater distance between us. "About ninety minutes from here!"

"Well," I said, continuing to press toward him, "tomorrow morning is Saturday, and I have nothing to do. How about I pick you up for breakfast and we travel there to see her? I really want to meet her."

At that, the teller of this scary story turned a flushed red, spun on his heels, and literally bolted out of the auditorium.

One of the ladies watching all of this posed the question to the other onlookers, "What was that all about?" Another lady spoke up saying, *"Didn't you pay attention to the seminar tonight? That guy was lying to us!"*

Exactly!

There are witches in the world, and those who practice witchcraft. There are followers of Satan, who make amazing claims and tell very disturbing stories. But what exactly are their powers?

Much of the misunderstanding of the truth behind Satan's powers stems from a misinterpretation of the nature of occult practices. To be sure, there are clear biblical directives that forbid participation in occult activities. For example, Deuteronomy 18:10-11 mentions sorcery, divination, enchantment, wizards, and witches. In this chapter we will take a close look at several biblical references to the Occult in order to "unmask" Satan's actual powers.

Sometimes translations of the original Hebrew or Greek language used in the Bible can confuse the intended meaning. This is due, in part, to the nature of the work of translation—as every translation requires interpretation. For example, two Hebrew words with different meanings are typically translated "sorcerer"; they are *kashap* and *anan*. The first, *kashap*, is commonly translated as "one who whispers spells." It is compared to adulterers, perjurers, and those who defraud laborers in Malachi 3:5. In Jeremiah 27:10 and Isaiah 57:3-4, *kashap* is used to describe those who are cheats, frauds, and liars. In Isaiah 47 we read that the work of the *kashap* fails.[77] *Kashap* has also been translated as "witch" or "witchcraft." This may mean that to be a witch, then, is to be one who whispers.

The second word found in the Old Testament that is translated "sorcerer" is *anan,* which in the Literal Bible is simply translated "a cloud reader." This translation is due to the primitive root of the word that means "to cloud over" (figuratively) or "to act covertly."

Note that the biblical definition of these terms does *not* include a descriptive such as "one who can wield miraculous powers," but rather the power behind this sorcery is cheating, fraud, whispering, or acting covertly. According to these biblical descriptions, then, occultists do not possess miraculous power. It may be that their power is the ability to deceive. Even in a contemporary definition of the word "sorcery," we should note the qualifiers to the use of the word. Here is Webster's definition of sorcery. He seems to be on to something:

sor-cer-y 1. The *supposed* use of an evil supernatural power over people and their affairs; witchcraft; black magic **2.** *Seemingly* magical power, influence, or charm.

The power of the sorcerer or the witch may be found in causing an individual to attribute incredible powers to himself or herself—powers that they may not actually possess. As Webster states, the sorcerer or witch may only have *supposed* powers and *seemingly* magical influence. This does not mean, however, that the power or influence is innocuous. It is still significant, and they could be under the influence of Satan or his demons, but whatever they exert could only be through their words and natural behavior, not the "miraculous"—a unique power that is attributed in the Scriptures solely to God.

The Hebrew word *nahash,* typically translated as "divination," is also interesting. This term refers to someone who *pretends* to have some secret knowledge. The term is ascribed to Joseph several times. From Old Testament scholar Robert Alden's *Theological Wordbook of the Old Testament*:

> *Both in Genesis 44:5 and 15 we learn that Joseph claimed for his brothers' benefit that he could 'divine' with a special cup and so knew secret things—such as that his brothers, still unaware of who he was, had his cup in their possession.*[78]

It appeared to his brothers that Joseph possessed supernatural insights; however, he was pretending. He knew where the cup was because he had it put there.

Another occult practitioner named in Deuteronomy 18 as the "charmer" is translated from the Hebrew term *habar*. The primary use of the term *habar* in the Old Testament refers to the "joining" or "uniting" of two or more objects. However, the root of the term includes the concept of "binding." This is specifically seen in the notion of "charm."

One more term from Deuteronomy 18:10-11 is the word translated "wizard." It may be the masculine form of "witch," as it is derived from the Hebrew word, *yidd'oni,* that always appears parallel to "witch" (Hebrew *'ob*). Both *yidd'oni* and *'ob* are associated with someone who calls on or worships the dead. The reference to "wizard" is sandwiched by the descriptives "consulting spirits" and "inquiring of the dead." Is this referring to genuine communication with the dead? Many biblical scholars believe it is deception, much like John Edward utilized in the television show *Crossing Over,* where he simulated communication with the dead for his viewers. As noted earlier in Chapter 6, Edward did provide a disclaimer at the conclusion of each program, for those astute enough to notice, that his work was to be considered "for entertainment purposes only. . . and not factual in any way whatsoever."[79]

Dr. Robert Alden, who earned his Ph.D. from the Hebrew Union College-Jewish Institute of Religion, points out that the prophet Isaiah understood the work of the witch or medium to be nothing more than the manipulation of their vocal cords in order to deceive.[80] Renowned Bible commentators, Merrill Unger and William White, also emphasize this inability of the medium to actually communicate with the dead.

> *Necromancers' unusual experiences do not prove that they truly had power to summon the dead. For example, the medium of Endor could not snatch Samuel out of God's hands against His wishes. But in this particular incident, it seems that God rebuked Saul's apostasy, either through a revived Samuel or through a vision of Samuel. [Or through a deception perpetrated by the witch.] Mediums do not have power to summon the spirits of the dead, since this is reprehensible to God and contrary to His will.*[81]

In Exodus 7:11, the magicians of Pharaoh also accomplished imitations of the genuinely miraculous. "Then Pharaoh also called the wise men and the sorcerers, and they also, the magicians of Egypt, did the same with their secret arts (*lahat*)." The Hebrew word for *lahat* refers to ensnaring people with secret practices.

Strong's definition of *lahat* suggests "a blaze," and the word is most typically translated "to kindle" or "to burn." This may suggest that the magicians had snakes enwrapped (*lahat*) in a hollow tube that had the appearance of a stick or a staff. Perhaps the tube was then set aflame (*lahat*) quickly, burning away the thin walls of the tube and leaving the snake in its place.

Regardless of the actual methodology, those who practiced occult rituals and apparent wonders never succeeded in performing genuine miracles. Throughout the Old Testament, one of the distinctions of the followers of Jehovah was their rejection of the claimed occult powers found amongst other people.

In striking contrast to her neighbors who were geniuses at creating a mythology, we find a perpetual tendency in Israel to demythologize life. Take for instance the word *lilith*, well known in this period as the Assyrian female night demon. In her one appearance in the Old Testament, she is included in a list of real animals and birds, with the jackals and wildcats, the pelicans, and the owls.

The same could be said for many other words which Israel used. The Old Testament acknowledges the spirit world but seems bent on minimizing, demythologizing, or marginalizing it. Wherever it does occur, it always has its origin in God (i.e., *Yahweh*) and its role and domain determined by His sovereignty. No autonomous domain, independent of *Yahweh*, or outside His immediate control, exists to threaten man.[82]

The idea here is similar to those who practice transcendental meditation in our day and claim to be able to levitate; however, they never actually perform any miraculous effect to defy the laws of gravity. Robert T. Carroll, author of *Becoming a Critical Thinker* and *The Skeptic's Dictionary*, made the following observation:

> *Levitation is the act of ascending into the air and floating in apparent defiance of gravity. Spiritual masters are often depicted as*

> *levitating and the ability to levitate is taken as a sign of blessedness by some. There are people in transcendental meditation who will sit cross-legged and hop up and down on their butts [sic], claiming that they are flying. Perhaps they are. . . for one-millionth of a second one millimeter above the ground. They say they feel lighter than air and are quite proud of their butt-hopping achievements.*[83]

New Testament references of the work and activity of the Satanic also support the fact that deception is being used, rather than genuine miraculous power. In 2 Thessalonians 2, the apostle Paul warns his readers to be on the lookout for self-proclaimed miracle workers in the end times. Note the italicized words [emphasis mine] that Paul connects to the work and activity of Satan:

> *Let no one in any way deceive you, for it will not come unless the apostasy comes first, and the man of lawlessness is revealed, the son of destruction, who opposes and exalts himself above every so-called god or object of worship, so that he takes his seat in the temple of God, displaying himself as being God. . . that is, the one whose coming is in accord with the activity of Satan, with all power and signs and false wonders, and with all the deception of wickedness for those who perish, because they did not receive the love of the truth so as to be saved.* (2 Thessalonians 2:3-4, 9-10 NASB)

John Anderson, author of *Psychic Phenomena Unveiled* and a former high priest of an occult group in California, affirms the instruction from 2 Thessalonians: "We should be alert to the identification of their feats as lying wonders and pay attention to the use of the adjective *lying*, or *false*, as opposed to the noun *wonders*."[84]

No autonomous domain, independent of Yahweh, or outside His immediate control, exists to threaten man.

In the end, only God can do the miraculous. Neither Satan, nor his army of demons, possesses the qualities or attributes of God. Angels are created beings and, fallen or not, do not possess the attributes of omnipresence, omniscience, or omnipotence (which includes the miraculous). Angels cannot prophecy the future apart from the involvement of the One who holds the future. All created beings are limited within the boundaries God has placed them. This is very different than what the average person believes of demonic activity.

Hollywood's interpretation of demons, the Devil, and the presumed powers of Satan are erroneously being adopted as consistent with Scripture. Too many movies attribute to Satan the ability to produce truly dramatic, sensational displays of occult phenomena.[85]

One passage that identifies the deceptive activity of Satan is Revelation 13:3, which states, "And I saw one of his heads *as if it had been slain*, and his fatal wound was healed. And the whole earth was amazed and followed after the beast." Note that the translators of the New American Standard Bible have used the phrase "as *if* it had been slain." They identify that what will take place is not a genuine resurrection.

In Exodus 15:11, Moses and the sons of Israel are found singing unto the Lord in rhetorical questions: "Who is like You among the gods, O Lord? Who is like You, majestic in holiness, Awesome in praises, working wonders [or working miracles]?" The obvious answer to that question is "No one!" In Psalm 72:18, Solomon declares, "Blessed be the Lord God, the God of Israel, Who *alone* works wonders." Then again, in Psalm 136:3-4, the psalmist proclaims, "Give thanks to the Lord of lords, for His lovingkindness is everlasting. To Him who *alone* does great wonders."

Notice that the attribute of God being praised is that God *alone* works wonders. The Hebrew word for "alone," *badad,* can also be expressed in the word "solitary." Dr. Louis Goldberg, former Professor of Theology and Jewish Studies at the Moody Bible

Institute in Chicago, IL, has written that the word "alone" as it appears in this passage "is used of the Lord's incomparability and uniqueness in His exclusive claim to deity as seen in his extraordinary works"[86] In other words, the reason why only God can perform the miraculous is that He alone is God.

There are and have been throughout history individuals who claimed to have miraculous powers and further claimed that their powers were from God (such as the late psychic, Jeane Dixon).[87] However, when God chooses to do the miraculous, He is very consistent in the pattern in which it is performed. God's pattern is enumerated by philosopher and theologian Dr. Norman Geisler as follows:

- Miracles are always successful
- Miracles are immediate
- Miracles have no relapses
- Miracles give confirmation of God's messenger.[88]

In addition to these four observations, God, rather than a person, is always glorified in the biblical examples of the miraculous. These patterns are found in every example of the genuinely miraculous as recorded in the Bible, and are helpful tools when encountering those who claim to be exercising a miraculous gift from God.

Let me repeat: In the end, only God can do the miraculous.

Chapter 17

DECEITFUL, DEVILISH, OR DIVINE?

"One of Satan's most deceptive and powerful ways of defeating us is to get us to believe a lie."
Dr. Charles Stanley

Identifying a Lie

The Bureau of Engraving in Washington, D.C. prints the currency of the United States. A huge production line of high tech printing presses overflows with sheets and sheets of dollar bills. One of the most obvious and serious responsibilities of the bureau is to produce bills that cannot easily be counterfeited, and many precautions are taken—such as micro printing patterns or characters on each bill that cannot be seen with the human eye, and maintaining a legal monopoly of the fabric on which the currency is printed. It is very difficult for the average person to spot or identify a counterfeit bill. Without knowledge, skills, or equipment to recognize "funny money," he or she is likely to accept it as genuine and value it as equal to the real thing.

That is why individuals with specialized training in spotting deception, such as illusionists and psychologists, are able to offer insights to unmask claimed paranormal phenomena when others, even those highly educated or trained in other fields, are unable to do so. For example, at Clark University in Worcester, Massachusetts, a symposium on psychical phenomena was held in 1926 featuring luminaries from such locations as Harvard, Leipzig, and Oxford. In attendance were Sir Oliver Lodge, Sir Arthur Conan Doyle (the famed author of Sherlock Holmes), and Dr. William McDougall to name a few; all of whom were "convinced of genuine psychical phenomena."[88]

L.R.G. Crandon, M.D., Boston physician and husband of the notorious medium Margery, made the following point in the concluding statement of his presentation. "The physical manifestations of the séance-room are real and valid sensorial experiences. Once that validity is established, the experiments will become respectable, and more data will pour in."[89]

The validity, however, was never established and the data never poured in. In fact, the data over subsequent decades refuted the conclusions of Crandon.[90] Two papers were submitted at Clark University that identified the deception of the claimed "psychical phenomena." They were written by famed magician, Harry Houdini, and psychologist Professor Joseph Jastrow. Both were experts in exposing the fraudulent activity of the spiritualists of their time. They candidly identified the connection between psychical activity and deception. An excerpt from Jastrow's paper is quoted here:

> *As soon as one type of performance is exposed another appears; but the point emerges that if any such claim is to be met and its examination conducted after the logical pattern of an experiment, then the one supreme condition is that the experimenter and not the medium shall control the conditions. That indispensable requirement is always evaded, though seemingly accepted. At the crudest we are told that light is inimical to these occult forces; so the shelter of darkness which nullifies the control is resorted to; or if not that, the screen of the table which conceals the modus operandi; or one is forbidden to stand at the only place from which the operation could be detected; and there are curtains and cabinets and holding of hands, and clever tricks of release from apparent control, and rigid examinations of the body which still leave a loophole of concealment; and ever the neglect of the observation that as such controls are made*

> *rigid, the phenomena are curtailed, while the amazing performances reported occur when such control is relaxed. . . . All this may sound dogmatic, when reduced to such curtness of statement; but the documentation is all too ample, and, to repeat, pathetic.*[91]

Dr. Norman Geisler concludes in his book, *Signs and Wonders*, that "in spite of Satan's super power, he cannot do truly supernatural things as God can do. For example, he cannot create life or raise the dead. . . . Satan does not need to be able to violate natural laws, as long as he can convince people he can do it. . . . He is not able to do true miracles, but he certainly can fool people into thinking that he can. So for all practical purposes his powers seem miraculous. Indeed, John speaks of "the spirits of demons performing miraculous signs" (Revelation 16:14). Inspired by Satan, the Antichrist will display "all kinds of counterfeit miracles, signs and wonders" (2 Thessalonians 2:9).[92]

Lessons from Job

John P. Newport, in his book *Satan and Demons: a Theological Perspective*, notes the following:

> *The most extensive Old Testament discussion of Satan is in Job. Here he is seen as God's agent and minister, who tested human fidelity. He makes a wager with God, with Job as the stake. He acts, however, with the express permission of God and keeps within the limits which God has fixed for him.*[93]

In the opening chapters of this ancient book, we find that Satan's request is being used to accomplish the purpose of God. It is Satan who made the request that God put forth His hand and touch all that Job had. Afterward, the "fire of God" fell from Heaven. The messenger who reported this sad news to Job believed that fire was a miraculous manifestation of God, not of Satan.

This was Job's understanding as well—and how he responded is fascinating. He fell to the ground and worshipped the Lord. He proclaimed that it is the Lord who gives and the Lord who takes away. Then the author of the book notes that Job did not sin in believing that the wrath came from the hand of God and that he did not "ascribe unseemliness to God" (Job 1:22). In other words, it was not inappropriate to understand that the catastrophic happenings were from God Himself.

A little later, God praised Job's response and confirmed that it was His power that brought catastrophe into Job's life when He spoke to Satan. "[Job] still holds fast his integrity, although you [Satan] incited Me against him," (Job 2:3). Then again, Satan made the request that God "put forth Thy hand" to touch Job's bone and flesh. In response, God then empowered Satan to do His bidding. Satan was unable to do anything on his own.

It is unpopular in today's Christian culture to suggest that disastrous things can come from the hand of God. Nevertheless, look carefully at Job 2:10 and consider Job's harsh but true words to his wife. "Shall we indeed accept good from God and not accept adversity?" In addition, the author of this historical narrative makes it clear that "In all this Job did not sin with his lips." Job was praised for understanding that his adversity was from God. Job understood that life and death and blessing and pain were all from the Lord. In Job 13:15, he declared, "Though He [God] slay me, I will hope in Him." In Job 16:11-12, he stated, "God hands me over to ruffians, and tosses me into the hands of the wicked. I was at ease, but He shattered me, and He has grasped me by the neck and shaken me to pieces."

Job did not understand why he received the trials which impacted his life so severely, but he did understand that the trials of his life were directly from God, in whom he could trust even when he didn't understand. This is the very heart of what it means to be a monotheist—trusting in the one true God of the universe even when we don't understand. God Himself declared this in other passages such as Deuteronomy 32:39, "See now that I, I am He, and there is no god besides Me; It is I who put to death and give life. I have wounded, and it is I who heal; and there is no one who can deliver from My hand."

The book of Job provides us with at least two basic understandings regarding Satan.

- **Satan is limited in his powers and actions.**

Theologian, John Newport, makes the following distinction:

> *It is clear that the Bible teaches that the power of the demonic is limited. Man can never be so totally corrupt that the forces of darkness have complete control over human history. The devil acts only within the limits set by the divine sovereignty. The devil is one whose power was originally granted to him by his Creator. We must beware of ascribing to Satan an authority which verges on the absolute.*[94]

- **Catastrophic destruction is not a normative practice of the devil.**

There is no biblical evidence that Satan can control natural phenomena or have supernatural authority over the physical nature of this world. Throughout Scripture, each account that speaks of supernatural involvement is attributed to God. No wonder Jesus used His miracles as an apologetic of His divine nature. In John 10:25; 37-38, Jesus said, "I told you, and you do not believe; the works that I do in My Father's name, these bear witness of Me. If I do not do the works of My Father, do not believe Me; but if I do them, though you do not believe Me, believe the works, that you may know and understand that the Father is in Me, and I in the Father."

Satan does not need to be able to violate natural laws, as long as he can convince people he can do it.

As important as it is to unmask deceit and expose the devil's deception, we must also learn to recognize the divine. When does an inexplicable event move from "strange coincidence" to the realm of the miraculous? Philosopher R. F. Holland defines a miracle as an event that is empirically certain (actually having occurred), conceptually impossible (inexplicable without appealing beyond our experience), and religious (calling for a spiritual explanation).[95] A more simplified definition is put forward by law professor and Christian apologist John Warwick Montgomery as "a unique, non-analogous occurrence."[96] Dr. Norm Geisler defines a genuine miracle as "a special act of God in the world, a supernatural interference into nature, a special divine intervention."[97] C.S. Lewis has said, "I use the word *Miracle* to mean an interference with Nature by supernatural power."[98] He went on to say:

> *Most stories about miraculous events are probably false: if it comes to that, most stories about natural events are false. Lies, exaggerations, misunderstandings and hearsay make up perhaps more than half of all that is said and written in the world. We must therefore find a criterion whereby to judge any particular story of the miraculous.*[99]

That is most assuredly true. It is best to understand the operation and activity of the supernatural realm primarily from Scripture, and then to be informed by those with expertise in identifying deception.

Why is this issue so important? Some would argue after all, if someone chooses to give more credit to Satan than he deserves, what harm is done? I can tell you, from interviewing many who have been involved in the occult, that it destroys lives.

However, the opposite is also true. When those who have been deceived by the lies of the occultist are able to discover and recognize the truth by unmasking the lies, they discover freedom and joy! It gives birth to life! I'll close my section of the book by sharing one of my favorite memories of seeing the power and the oppression of deception unmasked.

I was traveling to Louisiana to participate as one of the speakers at a large conference for families. About a week prior to my arrival, one of the pastors who was coordinating the event, called me to ask a favor. He shared with me that a young couple had started to attend his church, and that the young mother had come out of a rather difficult background, which included heavy involvement in the occult community. The couple, he observed, seemed to be genuine seekers of truth, but due to their dark background and experiences, they were literally "haunted" by their past. So, he asked if I would be willing to meet with them privately either before or after the conference to see if there was any way in which I could help or encourage them. Of course, I agreed.

Shortly after I arrived, I found myself seated at a restaurant table with a young and rather attractive couple. After a few pleasantries, I invited them to share with me a brief version of their life story.

I learned that they were, in fact, genuinely and authentically seeking to discover and learn more about Christian faith and understand what it means to live life from a biblical perspective. I learned that as new parents, they had become self-aware of the immense responsibility they now had in raising up their daughter – and doing so in a way that was, as they said, "spiritually healthy." From the tone of the young mom's voice, whom I will refer to as Bess (not her real name), I could tell she was implying that a spiritually healthy upbringing had not been her own experience.

Bess went on to share with me how she had grown up in the home of a medium. That was the practice and trade of her mother.

> "In the homes of all of my friends, the extra room in their houses was designated a guest room, or perhaps a TV room. In our house, the extra room was for séances." she said. "When I was home alone, and if the door was left open to that room, I was scared to even walk by it. I would lock myself in my bedroom."

"Did you ever participate in one of your mother's séances?" I asked.

"Yes, and it is one of my worst memories and recurring nightmares." As she shared this, her husband reached over and squeezed her hand, and affirmed to me that her fear was very real.

"Can you tell me about it?" I asked.

Over the next half-hour or so, Bess slowly and sometimes tearfully shared with me an experience that she had only talked of before to her husband and to her closest friend; an experience that had disturbed her and was the source of sleepless nights for over ten years.

She told me that as a child she was not permitted to attend the séances - all of which would take place in the late hours of the night. Her mother would send Bess to her room, while meeting with her "clients." From her room, however, Bess would hear strange noises and occasionally even screams coming from the séance parlor.

On the eve of Bess's thirteenth birthday, her mom announced that at midnight her uncles and aunt were coming over to the house to hold a special séance (kind of a Spiritualist's version of a Jewish bat mitzvah). Bess learned that she would participate in her first séance that night, as a rite of passage into the adult Spiritualist community.

At the stroke of midnight, seated at a round table in complete darkness with her mother, two uncles and her aunt, resting their hands palms-down on the table top - Bess's mom went into a trance and began calling upon the spirits of the dead. The young teen trembled as her mom's voice seemed to change and grow deeper, taking on a rather gravely tone to it.

There were long times of silence – waiting in the darkness for some sign of contact with the "other side."

The medium began to ask questions in the darkness. "Spirit, are you there?" And again, a long silence.

"Spirit, make yourself known to us with a sign" came the plea. Then it happened. The table at which they were seated seemed to move. At first, just a slight movement – so the medium queried, "Is that you Spirit?" And then the table literally lifted off the floor, with everyone's hands resting upon it. In fact, it became almost violent, as the table heaved up and down, while Bess's mom seemed to moan in some type of agony.

After just a minute or so (though Bess said it felt like an eternity), her mother collapsed forward on the table and everything stopped. One of the uncles turned on a light, and the ceremony was over.

All the color had drained from the face of Bess as she shared the story of her living nightmare with me. Her husband held her close. And once she had caught her breath, I said, "May I ask you a few questions about that terrible night?" "Yes, please" she responded.

So, I asked her, "How do you know that a spirit really appeared that night in your mother's parlor and lifted that table? How do you know that it wasn't just a trick?"

Bess responded to my questions by sharing with me that over the course of the years that followed her séance initiation, she spoke with her mother, uncles and aunt individually about that night, and they all swore that they were not involved in any type of trickery.

> "I want to ask you one more question Bess, and before I do, I want you to consider this. What you have described, if real, can only be described as a demonic miracle. Yet, according to my research and study of the Hebrew and Christian Scriptures, the only person able to perform such a miracle is God. So, how you answer this next

question, will either validate your mother's claim or the teachings of the Bible."

"And that question is?" Bess asked.

"When you think on the nature and character of your mother, your uncles, or your aunt – is there anything about them that would cause you to doubt whether or not they were capable of telling a lie? The difference between your experience being an authentic encounter with the spirit world, and an evil and seditious deception in order to instill fear and control, could be a lie."

Bess and her husband looked at each other as that thought settled in. And then, after a few moments, almost simultaneously, they both started to grin, and let out a large sigh of relief, as if to say "now we understand what happened that night." In fact, they started to laugh a little.

I said, "What is it about that question that strikes you as funny?"

"They are all compulsive liars!" Bess's husband blurted out. "They all lie all the time!" Bess confirmed.

In the complete darkness of that séance room, any one of her relatives could have been lifting the table up and down, completely unseen by Bess. In fact, Bess shared that her eyes were squeezed as tightly closed as she could keep them throughout the entire ordeal. Each of them was capable of perpetrating a hoax and then lying about it later. But the experience was so intense, that neither Bess, nor her husband, had ever made the connection before that her relatives were just telling another lie; something they were all known to do quite regularly.

As the realization sunk in that her fear was sourced in accepting a lie as a reality, you could almost see the weight of that emotional burden falling from her shoulders as the deception of the séance parlor room of ten years ago was unmasked.

Now, the long-held fears of a traumatic childhood experience such as this, don't just instantly disappear when the lie is exposed and the truth is discovered. But today, that young couple can live without fear of the "dark forces" her deceitful family members promoted, and can live in the light of the truth! To paraphrase John 8:32, "when you know the truth, the truth will make you free!"

Remember Job? If we can model his attitude—trusting in God for all things—and keep our eyes fixed on Him who drives out all fear, then we can be confident that we are not living in the *illudere*, but living in the confidence of the one true God.

Section Three

Unmasking the Miracles of Jesus

Adrian Van Vactor

Some have claimed that Jesus of Nazareth was simply a highly skilled magician, not a real miracle worker. Others say long-recounted stories of His miracles were simply myths to be dismissed to the dust bin of countless other mythical narratives. Still others say He was and is Messiah—the one true worker of real miracles, especially in people's lives and in life-transforming ways. In this final section, illusionist Adrian Van Vactor recounts his personal search for the truth about Jesus: myth, magician, or miracle-working Messiah?

Adrian Van Vactor

About Adrian Van Vactor

Adrian Van Vactor is an internationally known award-winning illusionist and Christian apologist with FaithSearch International. As a teenager, he was honored by many of the world's greatest magicians when they awarded him the Milbourn Christopher Newcomer Award, voting him the "most promising young magician of the future." Earlier that year, he was awarded the coveted Lance Burton Award, competing in Las Vegas against some of the most talented young illusionists from around the world. Adrian has been working professionally in the field of illusion since 1992.

Van Vactor toured for many years with "The André Kole Magical Spectacular," and has conducted over fifty international tours in twenty-seven countries on six continents, sharing the Gospel with hundreds of thousands of high school and college youth through the art of illusion. He has headlined at the world-famous Magic Castle in Hollywood, California and was invited to speak and perform for over 11,000 people at the World's Fair in Hanover, Germany. Adrian has been humbled to present the gospel and see tens of thousands of men, women, and children commit their lives to Christ through his illusion performances. His travels have also given him the opportunity to debunk psychic surgeons in South Asia, witch doctors in Africa, and self-proclaimed psychics in just about every corner of the Earth.

Van Vactor worked for many years with Youth for Christ and Campus Crusade for Christ International, through which he received extensive evangelism training as a graduate of CRU's Communication Center. Adrian also studied at the Billy Graham School of Evangelism.

Adrian is president and founder of Adrian Van Vactor International Ministries (www.avvim.org), whose mission is "to utilize the art of illusion as a tool to bridge cultural and generational gaps and communicate the Gospel of Jesus Christ." Currently he is on tour with his original production, "Secrets of the Supernatural Exposed", a very entertaining and engaging multi-media presentation that gives the audience an informative and refreshing look at the supernatural.

(Learn more about Adrian Van Vactor at www.avvim.org.)

Chapter 18
A Sacred Quest

"The pursuit of truth and beauty is a sphere of activity in which we are permitted to remain children all our lives."
Albert Einstein

Childhood can be a wondrous time, full of mystery and fantasy. It's the only time in your life you are permitted to believe and enjoy the unbelievable... the fairytale. For many children, those moments of mystery and fantasy often enjoyed at Christmas and Easter bring welcome relief from a painful and unstable reality.

My childhood, like so many others experience, was filled with a lot more reality than fantasy, and more pain than mystery. As the son of a Vietnam veteran during a time when little was known about Post Traumatic Stress Disorder, much less how to treat it, my biggest fantasy was just having a relationship with my father. Understandably, the only way he could muffle the pain and sorrow from the horrors of war was on a bar stool, which kept him isolated from our mother, me, and my two younger siblings.

My father left us when I was seven. Even though his personal struggles brought chaos to our home, he was my dad and being separated from him was unbearable; so much so, that I would run away to find him. After court drama, tears, and heartache, in the end it was the will of a boy who just wanted to be with his father that won. When I finally moved in with my dad he had already remarried; his new family came with four older stepchildren, and I was the outsider. Of course, his issues were still a large factor in our home. However, it was those unstable relationships in a very broken and dysfunctional family that ultimately led me, not only toward my interest in magic, but toward my inevitable pursuit of truth and faith.

Child Meets Myth

With all the obstacles I lived with, there was one moment, every year that I just loved and made me feel normal—Christmas. Mixed with my large dose of reality, Christmas still held just enough fantasy to keep the kid in me alive. Christmas was where the magic awaited me. I always had an eager anticipation of Santa's arrival. I imagined the jolly ol' elf moving quietly about the dimly lit living room as he set out the gifts for morning. I would stay awake for as long as I could to see if I could catch him taking a bite of a cookie. Each year my grin was only widened by the fact that my visitations with my mom and younger siblings gave me TWO Christmases! A child's wonder… there is nothing quite like it.

When I was nine, I saw a magician perform a live illusion show and decided that I wanted to be just like him—creating a sense of wonder for others. Honestly, I wasn't all that fooled by the tricks; I was always the kid who asked a lot of logical questions and tried to figure things out. As I watched him perform, I asked myself queries that few other children ever considered. I was insatiably curious. If I had been on Dorothy's crew in the Emerald City of Oz, I would've been the one to pull back the curtain. I was a natural skeptic with an investigative mind.

As physicist Michio Kaku said, "We are born scientists; when we're born, we wonder what's out there. . . ."[100] For me, the natural world seemed fairly self-explanatory, so it was the mythical world of fantasy and storytelling that became a hidden interest as I entered adolescence. To keep the magic going and that inner wonder alive, I developed a wild, nerdy imagination. Of course, that made me a target for cruelty from my three older stepbrothers. The allure of pulling off the "miracles" I'd seen professional magicians perform became more and more enticing, and it was a skill I thought could bring me the acceptance I longed for, as well as an escape from a painful home reality.

Child Meets Magician

By the time I was thirteen years old, I had been dabbling in the art of illusion for several years, using magic books from the local library and once even putting on an impromptu show for my grandparents. These exploits did indeed help me deal with bullying and improve my image in my stepbrothers' eyes, but a whole new world opened to me when I met a real live magician. Gene was my barber as well as a skilled illusionist. From the day he pulled a coin from my ear, I was hooked. A few months later, Gene helped me to become the youngest member of the Society of American Magicians' Tucson chapter, one of the larger chapters in the world at that time that ultimately became the launching pad for my full-time career.

During that first year as I trained to become a professional magician, I was exposed to three different types of paranormal phenomena: Ouija boards, tarot cards, and psychic channeling. It didn't take long for me to conclude a basic natural explanation for these phenomena. One day my sister and her friend were playing with a homemade Ouija board, and it frightened them. To demonstrate why and how the board worked, I tied a ball to a string and shared how to make the ball "move with your mind" by imagining it swinging in slight patterns. It was a simple but effective demonstration of the ideomotor effect.[101] I also explained that it was impossible for game participants to get any meaningful message if they were blindfolded. I was not convinced that the planchette moved on its own and wanted to make sure my sister and her friend shared my doubt.

For a brief time, my dear sweet mother dallied with the New Age movement craze of the 1980s. It gave me the opportunity to explain to her how psychics did cold readings after she insisted I sit and watch self-proclaimed medium, J. Z. Knight, summon the spirit Ramtha. I was not in the slightest bit impressed—especially since the spirit-god kept losing its English accent! I knew it was a scam, and my mom left the New Age movement shortly thereafter.

My first magician's meeting, my first stage performance, and my first psychic debunk all occurred in 1987 and 1988, along with puberty, freshman year in high school, and the discovery of girls. Talk about a magical year! Although it was fun to figure out how Ouija boards and cold readings worked, psychic claims weren't the only thing I discovered at that time. I was also introduced to Jesus of Nazareth and met my first Christians.

Child Meets Messiah

My mother was raised as a Catholic in Nogales, Mexico, but I didn't know a thing about Jesus except for my erroneous perceptions. I thought of Him as a white Spanish-speaking man from Mexico depicted hanging on a wooden cross who, after His death, had light floating all around Him. Before I moved in with my father, I spent half of second grade in Catholic school and was taken to Mass when I visited my grandparents in Mexico.

Of course, my Latino heritage is not to blame for not knowing Jesus. I didn't know I was allowed to ask questions about the eerie, dark candle lights and strong incense I saw as a child during night Mass. My grandparents were simply doing what they thought was right. I likely would've continued going to Mass and Catholic school had my parents not divorced when I was seven. There was virtually no faith in my father's home; my father and stepmother possessed a strong anti-religious sentiment, and I was encouraged by the few friends that I did have to doubt God's existence. To this day, my father is an atheist.

Still, as a young man, God's existence just made sense to me, even though, at that time in my life, I lacked empirical proof of the Creator Himself. The Big Bang theory was pretty well established, and the Principle of Causality—that any one thing that comes into being or existence (the effect) must have a cause—was common sense enough for me to know there had to be some sort of first and necessary cause for the Big Bang to occur. Plus, the human mind, our relational nature, and our need to love and be loved seemed evidence enough to me that the cause of the Big Bang was a Creator that was both intelligent and personal.

Intuitively, I understood life had meaning, purpose, and objective moral values. I knew that my life choices and actions were genuine and either right or wrong. Within atheism, I did not see an objective basis to maintain these values. Only within belief in the existence of a god or gods could such purpose and meaning exist.

Still, there is a big difference between a general belief in the existence of God and having a relationship with Jesus Christ. My exposure to the claims of Jesus as recorded in the Bible came from a few Christian magicians I got to know as a teen. Rod Robison, author of this book, was one of them. The stories about Jesus seemed to make sense, and I even talked to God every now and then. When I was sixteen, one of my magic teachers, Allan, invited me to attend his church. I don't recall what the pastor's sermon was about, but I do remember the moment when he asked for people to come forward to the front of the platform if they wanted to become a Christian—because my legs compelled me forward. I was the only one of hundreds of people there that morning to respond.

My newfound faith was not as well received in my anti-religious home. Although I was often ridiculed, I stood my ground on the basics of my new faith; God was real, I assumed Jesus was real, and I knew God wanted me to be a good person. Still, I was only mildly committed since my understanding was minimal. It wasn't until I had a more personal encounter with God at age nineteen that my faith had a life-altering impact.

I was driving on Interstate 10 on my way to headline at The Magic Castle in Hollywood on the Palace of Mystery stage. I was listening to a preacher on the radio, and his words so penetrated my heart that for the first time I felt a desire to actually connect with God. He was no longer just "out there" somewhere; I needed to be real with God, give my life over to Him, and come clean about my thoughts, attitudes, and deeds. Over the following weeks, I called every person I had ever wronged, confessed the worst of my secret hidden sins, and tried to make amends for all of my offenses.

True to my logical thinking, I also became even more skeptical of paranormal claims. Show me a video of a psychic channeling a spirit, a ghost hunter show, or some miracle-performing guru and I could usually figure out the "secret" of what they were doing. I also realized that their extraordinary claims could be easily written off as hearsay or myth. I even became increasingly critical of miraculous claims from those of my own faith.

This prompted me to ask myself, "If I am so skeptical about all things paranormal, how is it that my belief in Jesus is an exception?" Was my encounter that night on Interstate 10 just an emotional experience where I allowed my hope in a Heavenly Father to fill the void left by my relationally absent earthly father? Perhaps my faith in God somehow filled a need to be liked, or maybe boosted my ego and self-esteem by providing me a truth that no one else around me accepted. Maybe I was simply being duped by the stories. I wondered if I had placed too much trust in the people I admired who shared their faith with me at the magic society.

Child Goes on a Quest

Only one year after my experience with God on the freeway, I needed to know if there was any rational foundation for my Christian faith. I was touring with André Kole and living the dream as his tech director. I handled all of the lights and sounds, taped down hundreds of feet of cables, crawled in catwalks, and singed my hands on hot stage lamps in theaters and churches across the country. I also performed my act as a guest performer in André's show.

Those years on the road were probably the most stressful I've experienced. On top of my other duties, there was the pressure each night of getting my act ready. Famous magician Vito Lupo once told me, "Your act is like three hours of magic crammed into six minutes." Those six minutes took a lot of prep. The drive to each new city, however, did provide ample time to create new ideas for my show, think, and look more deeply into my beliefs in God and the Bible.

About a month or two into my spiritual investigation, a friend and I who were performing magic together in the Dallas area decided to go see a movie. On our way back from the theater, we started talking about faith. I was transparent about my beliefs and my questions about it, and he told me that he had once attended seminary school. He shared how he, too, had traveled down a path of faith as a young person. For about twenty minutes, he delivered a polite and sincere lecture about how I needed to remain open-minded and not be too dogmatic about issues of faith. I couldn't comprehend why on Earth anyone would not be dogmatic. "If something is true," I reasoned, "we should act accordingly."

Then he said something that lit a fire within me. "You're young," he said with a double-dog-dare smirk on his face. "You'll get over it eventually."

I was taken aback by that comment. It made me feel as if I was just in a phase, or that I hadn't thought things through. I welcomed the challenge, though, because all I usually did in my spare time was think. I decided to set the record straight. I was determined to apply the same curiosity and skepticism I used in discerning psychic phenomena and magic tricks to an examination of the person of Jesus Christ.

So I set out on a sacred quest. Over many months, even years, I continually challenged myself and affirmed my commitment to an honest critique of Jesus and the concept of faith. I analyzed opposing worldviews, various paranormal claims, even the claims of the major faiths of the world. This absolute commitment to an honest critique brought me back full circle to my upbringing and my strained relationship with my father. Even though he struggled to be in my life emotionally as he coped with his own demons, there was one lesson he taught me that I will always remember and be thankful for.

Nothing could make my father angrier than dishonesty. Whenever we were caught in a lie, he would say in the most stern gaze, "I don't care what you do with your life, just always tell the truth." I took that challenge even further. I would only hold onto that which *proved* to be true, wherever possible and regardless of how it made me feel. I learned to find the truth by exposing that which proved to be false. As the magicians who are the authors of this book have had to do, I knew I needed to unmask the masquerade of my own personal superstitions and faith.

In the chapters that follow, I will take you along on my quest. Before we begin, I will let you in on a little secret; it's now been twenty-three years since that conversation in Dallas. As André Kole has often said when referring to the skeptics in his own life, "I haven't gotten over it yet."

Chapter 19
MYTH, MAGICIAN, OR MESSIAH?

"You must make your choice. Either this man was, and is, the Son of God, or else a madman or something worse."
C.S. Lewis

Having been on the road since I was nineteen years of age, gas stations, airports, and truck stops have been a constant of my existence. On my very first tour as a magician, I put fourteen thousand miles on my little Chevy pick-up truck in one month.

During the early years, I also didn't have the travel gadgetry that we take for granted today. Whether in the good ol' U.S. of A. or somewhere else on the planet, I was limited to a calling card and my trusty Rand McNally map. When traveling internationally, I didn't have a laptop or a smartphone, so tracking down an Internet café to communicate back home was common. To date, I've been on fifty-four international tours, and I've seen and met some interesting people.

Real-Life Guru

I recall one memorable encounter during one of my tours in South Asia. I was in an airport Internet café typing away at one final email prior to flying out to my next city. I hit "send," logged out, and ran to my gate. I barely made it to the last shuttle taking passengers across the tarmac to board the aircraft. Only one other person was with me, and I recalled seeing him earlier in the café. We both looked at one another and were likely thinking the same thing—we cut that one real close.

"Where are you from?" I asked.

"Chicago," he exclaimed over the loud rumble of the shuttle bus. His accent led me to conclude he wasn't originally from the Midwest, so I probed a little further.

"Where are you originally from?" He mentioned a South American country. I'm fairly fluent in Spanish, so I said in that language, "Oh wow! What brings you here?"

He told me he was on his way back to America after attending a conference. That piqued my curiosity. Having been to South Asia many times before, I had a hunch that it was unlikely for a man from South America who lives in Chicago to have traveled halfway around the world for merely a conference. I suspected a bit of misdirection on his part.

"What kind of conference would bring you here?" I asked him. This prompted him to reveal that he was in the country to see Sathya Sai Baba, the renowned guru-godman.

"Ah, I know who he is," I said. "I've been to his main compound three times." He perked up immediately, assuming he had run into a fellow believer. With a big smile on his face, he testified that the retreat was inspirational and life-changing. He held up his hand and showed me a ring on his finger. It had a cross on it. He was positively giddy. "He materialized this for me!"

To fully appreciate the man's excitement, you need to understand a bit more about Baba. He was a guru in India who has since died, but in his lifetime he made the outrageous claim of being all gods of all religions, including the reincarnate Jesus Christ. He "proved" his claims by making various kinds of jewelry appear out of nowhere, including necklaces and rings with crosses on them as a not-so-subtle reminder that he was the same Jesus from the first century. You can still find shops in the cities he frequented that sell pictures of him and key chains with a picture of the traditional Catholic image of Jesus Christ on one side and Baba's on the other.

It just so happened that I had a Morgan Silver Dollar coin that I used to practice my sleight-of-hand techniques. After he told me of the miracle materialization, I responded, "Oh, kinda like this?" I reached into the air and made the coin "miraculously" appear right in front of him. I wish I'd had a camera to capture his stunned look. I suspect he may have thought that Baba had granted me his power. Puzzled, he asked, "Why are you here?"

"I am an illusionist. I travel around the world explaining to university students why Baba and others like him are not who they claim to be."

"Oh yeah?" he retorted. "Uh—I'm sure it's some kind of sleight of hand."

He was now grappling with the realization that there was a good chance that Baba, a jovial and mysterious guru with millions of followers across the globe, may have deceived him. He tried to defend his experience. "The important thing is that it's motivational. He is simply trying to inspire people and improve their lives."

I paused a moment, and then questioned, "How is something inspirational when the whole thing is based on a lie?"

"Well, it's just for motivation, that's all." Our shuttle arrived at the aircraft, and he quickly got up and boarded the aircraft. It was obvious he didn't want to continue our chat.

Futile Faith

I have to agree with Paul the Apostle. When writing to the Christian Church in Corinth, he confronted the claim that the dead never come back to life. He reasoned that if that were true, then even Jesus could not have come back from the dead—and if Jesus never came back to life, then all Christians who follow Him "are the most pitiable people of all" for having believed such a tale.[102] This believer in Baba fell into that camp. If the very evidence for his claims is false, then that invalidates his claim. We're back to the fact that Baba was just a man, though certainly a clever one.

Human beings will go to great lengths to find faith, inspiration, and transcendence in hopes of discovering that there is more to this life than what we see, hear, taste, touch, and smell. The existential struggle, after all, is understandable. Many of us, especially in secular Western culture, live life in a way that suggests we see ourselves as free agents who value personal experience and responsibility. We feel we have the freedom to determine our destiny and have a moral responsibility to do so. Yet, this belief is in direct conflict with the pervasive secular teaching that our random chance origin ends with an unavoidable fate in a seemingly deterministic and meaningless universe. So, we struggle. We are not truly satisfied with the theory that nature is all there is, that our genetic make-up *determines* who we are, what we'll do, and how we will think. We reach for more, because this line of reason leads to complete hopelessness, a dark and destructive destination. So, it's perfectly understandable to want to believe in life after death, in a loving Creator, or other transcendent and eternal concepts that give life more meaning, purpose, and value.[103]

High Stakes

Though I have pity for a person if they believe a known lie, I don't fault them for desiring some sort of metaphysical hope in life. The ones I do fault are the peddlers of lies who will stop at nothing to give people false hope for profit, fame, or other contemptible gain. Baba was filthy rich as a result of his claim to divinity. It's the same old game—the exploitation of vulnerable people in search of real hope and answers to life's ultimate questions.

André Kole had a great opening line to his program. "Ever since the beginning of time, ever since there have been people in the world to be deceived, there have been always been people to deceive them. Sometimes they are called magicians, other times they are called politicians."[104] It's funny, but it's also sadly true.

I never saw my Sai Baba enthusiast again after our brief airport encounter, but it wasn't the first or the last time I would run into a true believer in Baba. In that same country I performed many times, with the goal of bringing both Baba's trickery and the hope and truth of Christianity into the light. One such event I performed in a sort of community center where Baba would hold some of his meetings to bless his followers with his supposed miracles. I was required to stand on the opposite side of the room from where Baba would stand, with all of the audiences chairs turned around. Surprisingly, though, I was permitted to present my entire program, including my subtle debunking of Baba!

I performed some of Baba's tricks and shared that there were many people throughout the world who could perform these same effects. In contrast to my program, I explained, these other performers would claim that their effects were real miracles. I then upstaged my imitation of Baba's tricks with a more impressive illusion and explained again that these were just special effects anyone can learn. I dared not ever mention Baba's name specifically, for I would certainly have been mobbed. But, my reference to him was clear enough that I could always hear whispers in the audience, "Sai Baba... Sai Baba." My presentation managed to keep my audience at peace, even though nearly every audience member in every performance in that country would have had tremendous reverence for the man.

After this particular performance, a woman in the Brahmin caste of the Hindu faith approached me. She obviously was a very highly respected woman for, as soon as she began to speak, the surrounding crowd went somewhat silent in anticipation of what she was about to say. "You're talking about Sai Baba, aren't you," she exclaimed. I reluctantly and gently said, "Yes, I'm referring to Sai Baba." Her facial expression went from the "Ah-ha, I'm on to you" sort to one of the saddest expressions I think I have ever seen. Her countenance changed dramatically at the realization that what she had put her faith in was quite possibly a sham of epic proportions.

Adrian Van Vactor's conversation with the Brahmin woman at the community center.

Whether you consider yourself a person of faith or not, an honest question to ask is, "What makes Jesus any different than the Babas of the world today?" It's easy to debunk a guru with a strong following. It's even easier to expose a deceptive television psychic. However, if we are to be consistent, why not put the most important and influential "miracle worker" of all time, Jesus Christ, to the test? After all, with titles such as "King of Kings," "Lord of Lords," and "God with us," it's monumentally important that we not ignore asking the same questions of Jesus as we would of any other claimant to the supernatural. "Who are you—really?"

Setting the Stage

If magicians were to unmask Jesus the same way we reveal modern "fakers," what would we find? Would we find that those who believe that Jesus rose from the dead are to be pitied for their naïve belief? Before we can unmask Jesus, we need a reliable record of His life. In the process of discovering and examining that record, we will explore three options.

First, we will examine the more predominant view among skeptics by attempting to unmask the miraculous accounts of Jesus as mere misconceptions and outright fabrications of history that have shaped our understanding of who He really was. Is it possible that there are myths of a miracle-working Jesus (the Jesus of faith) that have become so ingrained in the mindset of western religious civilization that they have overshadowed the actual facts of Jesus' historical life (Jesus of history)? Do we have good reasons for believing He even existed at all? If we do, is the first century Jesus anything like the Jesus who Christians believe in today?

Second, once we establish a reasonable portrait of Jesus, we will attempt to unmask Jesus as a master of the art of deception. Was He nothing more than a first century magician who pulled off the greatest illusion of all time—starting the world's largest religion that still claims 2.2 billion believers today? If so, then He should be seen as a clever trickster, but certainly not as the Messiah.

Finally, we will explore if there are any good reasons for having faith in Jesus as the actual Messiah, the God-incarnate Savior of the world, and share additional thoughts on the viability of faith while living in the modern scientific age.

Van Vactor performing on tour in South Asia

Chapter 20
THE MASK OF MYTH

"If you look for truth, you may find comfort in the end; if you look for comfort you will not get either comfort or truth only soft soap and wishful thinking to begin, and in the end, despair."
C.S. Lewis

Since I spend a lot of time talking about the subject of magic during my programs, critics of my more skeptical approach who believe in the paranormal often try to challenge me. Their objection is that I cannot use my skeptical method to disprove their respective experiences. One can't deny a person's experiences without some sort of evidence that can positively counter the claim. My reply to this objection is that while I am challenging their *interpretation* of what they think happened, I am not claiming that they didn't have *some sort* of experience; that is, I'm not saying they are delusional or lying.

After many of my programs, audience members inundate me with stories of paranormal encounters. Others, usually university students, want me to explain a specific phenomenon they have heard about themselves. Whether it is an encounter with a person channeling a so-called "spirit" or a witch doctor or godman performing some sort of apparent miracle, the stories usually have two commonalities:

1. **A level of vagueness** that warrants skepticism as to the origin of the story (such as no one actually saw the event). Most people who share a story of the paranormal were not actual eyewitnesses of the events. Without an eyewitness account, it's like trying to debunk how Hercules performed his feats of strength.
2. **A lack of confidence** in the story being preserved as the events actually took place. It's easy for critical facts of a paranormal event to get embellished or omitted.

As a skeptic with a desire to be an honest critical thinker, my approach is simple. I want to know the source of the story: I ask *who, what, when,* and *where* type of questions. If there are eyewitnesses, I next ask if they are still alive. If they are, I challenge the person sharing the story with me to take me to visit the witness. After all, why would I want to hear someone's second-hand account?

A few years back while I was on tour in Australia, I was performing my show and giving a talk at the University of Queensland. During my "magic" disclaimer (the part in the program where I explain to students that what I do as a magician is nothing more than scientific investigation and clever hand manipulation), I performed a quick cold reading for a woman in the audience. I did this to demonstrate how easy it is to give the illusion of having psychic powers to someone who is a complete stranger. I should note that the person I performed the cold reading on was absolutely convinced that I was genuinely psychic. In her view, I could not have said what I said by mere logical commonalities, inference, or lucky guessing.

Even after two years, upon returning to that campus, my hosts told me that she was still baffled and often talked about our encounter. She eventually concluded I was not psychic but that her brother was playing a prank on her by giving me the information. This painfully illustrates how individuals will not accept just how clever and sophisticated magicians, psychics, and the like are.

During my question and answer time after the performance, a student asked my opinion about a psychic he knew who was apparently able to see people's diseases, offer remedies psychically over the telephone, and see their futures and give counsel on what decisions to make. The student did not fully explain what he had personally experienced with this psychic, but he openly confessed that he had doubts that the psychic's abilities were genuinely supernatural.

My first question was, "Are you an eyewitness?" The student claimed that he had indeed personally witnessed the psychic doing some strange things he could not explain.

"Okay, let's go put the psychic to the test," I said. "How long will it take us to drive to her house?"

Most people at this point shrug and walk away, but it turned out this psychic was the student's mother. We exchanged contact information, and I eventually talked to her. She was unwilling to submit to my tests to prove the validity of her abilities. "If you were a real psychic," I explained to her over the phone, "you should have no problem passing my simple tests. I believe it's your obligation to provide your son with genuine proof." But she felt she didn't need to prove anything to anyone. My guess is she realized she would be caught in a lie in front of her son.

Putting a present-day claimant to the test and proving that someone's supposed supernatural ability is actually trickery or illusion is one thing, but how do you disprove claims that a person from history never existed, or that stories of his powers were myth instead of truth? Specifically, how do we address those who doubt the miracles of Jesus?

Chapter 21

UNMASKING THE JESUS MYTH HYPOTHESIS

If there is one fable, which would seem entitled to escape the analysis, which we have undertaken of religious poems and sacred legends. . . it is doubtless that of Christ. . . ."
Charles François Dupuis, 18th Century Jesus Mythicist

Many supposed experts will say that all you will find in an investigation of the life of Jesus Christ is a fictional character with no connection to any real person that existed, or that Jesus is a fairy tale invention mimicking the classic pagan "god born as man" epics.

It's understandable that some scholars conclude that the true Jesus of history has been muddled up over the centuries. Yet there are also those who conclude that all of the stories of Jesus are myth. Entire websites are devoted to such a view. Most modern scholars, though, place the "all myth" hypothesis on the same level of credibility as the claims of the Flat Earth Society.

Popular New Testament critic Bart Ehrman says that "despite this enormous range of opinion, there are several points on which virtually all scholars of antiquity agree. Jesus was a Jewish man, known to be a preacher and teacher, who was crucified (a Roman form of execution) in Jerusalem during the reign of the Roman emperor Tiberius when Pontius Pilate was the governor of Judea. Even though this is the view of nearly every trained scholar on the planet, it is not the view of a group of writers who are usually labeled, and often label themselves, mythicists."[105]

Ehrman went on to say in a *Huffington Post* article promoting his book *Did Jesus Exist? The Historical Argument for Jesus of Nazareth*, "With respect to Jesus, we have numerous, independent accounts of his life in the sources lying behind the Gospels (and the writings of Paul)—sources that originated in Jesus' native Aramaic tongue and that can be dated to within just a year or two of his life."[106]

When I first began my quest to uncover the validity of the miraculous claims of Jesus in as unbiased and objective a manner as I could, I knew I couldn't approach it in the exact same manner as I would with a modern paranormal claimant. I couldn't question any living eyewitnesses. That meant my investigation would have to be of a primarily historical nature. However, if there were historical archives of credible eyewitness accounts, I could use those to dig as a magician for deceptive clues regarding His miracles, death, and resurrection.

Flavius Josephus and other external sources

Before I could discover if there are any credible eyewitness accounts of Jesus' life, I had to find if there is evidence that He even existed at all.

Josephus' story is a fascinating one. He was a first century Jewish priest (Pharisee) who later became a soldier and fought in the great Jewish war against the Romans (66 A.D.). In 67 A.D., he surrendered to the Romans and was taken prisoner. He predicted that his captor, General Vespasian, would become emperor in what may have been an attempt to lengthen his life.[107] Fortunately for Josephus, his prediction came true. Vespasian became emperor in 69 A.D., and Josephus gained his freedom and changed his name to Flavius.

After the siege of Jerusalem (70 A.D.), during which Flavius acted as an interpreter for Vespasian's son Titus (who later succeeded his father as emperor), Flavius moved to Rome where he was given Roman citizenship and a pension. Flavius then devoted his life to his literary works, including his twenty-volume work, *Antiquities of the Jews*, completed around 93 or 94 A.D. In it, he makes a reference to Jesus Christ:

> *Now, there was about this time Jesus, a wise man, if it be lawful to call him a man, for he was a doer of wonderful works—a teacher of such men as receive the truth with pleasure. He drew over to him both many of the Jews, and many of the Gentiles. He was [the] Christ; and when Pilate, at the suggestion of the principal men amongst us, had condemned him to the cross, those that loved him at the first did not forsake him, for he appeared to them alive again the third day, as the divine prophets had foretold these and ten thousand other wonderful things concerning him; and the tribe of Christians, so named from him, are not extinct at this day.*[108]

Some scholars believe that this passage was later supplemented by a follower of Jesus who added the words "if it be lawful to call him a man" and "He was [the] Christ."[109] Nevertheless, I picked up my own copy of *The Works of Josephus: Complete and Unabridged* from a used bookstore and found the existence of this passage to be profound. In addition, there exists an Arabic translation of this work, considered to be a translation of the original text of Josephus *before* Christian influence, that also contains the widely accepted and slightly shorter version of this passage that retains most of what was said in the version quoted above.[110] Jesus is again mentioned in *Antiquities of the Jews* in a passage that, to my knowledge, no Flavius Josephus scholar questions as to its authenticity:

> *Festus was now dead, and Albinus was but upon the road; so he assembled the Sanhedrin of judges, and brought before them the brother of Jesus, who was called Christ, whose name was James, and some others, [or, some of his companions]; and when he had formed an accusation against them as breakers of the law, he delivered them to be stoned.*[111]

Whenever I had dialogues with skeptics about the existence of Jesus, I was given the impression that the only references to Jesus were from the Bible itself, and to use the New Testament as a reference was mere circular reasoning. I had no idea that a source external to the Bible would be a Jewish historian writing within one eyewitness generation of the events surrounding Jesus' life. In fact, as I continued through my research, I was surprised at the number of references to Jesus and early Christians there are from ancient historians, philosophers, and government officials (Tacitus, Suetonius, Thallus, Pliny the Younger, Emperor Trajan, Emperor Hadrian, Lucian, and Mara Bar-Serapion to name a few) dating from the late first century into the second century.[112] This evidence points to a real person in history, Jesus, who began a movement and gained a historically noteworthy following. In addition, two-thirds of these sources mention Jesus' death and His miracles. Some even talk about His resurrection and appearing to His disciples.

Saul of Tarsus

Usually the most compelling testimony comes from a person who was once against a belief that they now hold. Saul was a zealous Jew trained in the highest levels of Judaism and a known persecutor of the early Christian Church. One to two years after the death of Jesus, Saul had a traumatic encounter with a risen Jesus while he was on his way to arrest more of Jesus' followers. This experience not only changed Saul's mind about his mission to quell this heretical movement, but he himself also became a convert. No doubt his experience forced Saul to rethink his entire Jewish perspective on the new Jesus movement and his own theological understandings. If Jesus never existed, who then was Saul persecuting? Followers of whom?

Saul changed his name to Paul and became an apostle of the movement, penning two-thirds of the New Testament. The writings of Paul date as some of the earliest sources of Christianity.

Rubens' "The Conversion of St. Paul": courtesy of www.peterpaulrubens.org[158]

One particular and very notable Christian creed[114] discovered by historical Jesus scholars to have been recited by the apostle was also found in 1 Corinthians 15:3-7:

> *For I passed on to you as most important what I also received: that Christ died for our sins according to the Scriptures, that he was buried, that he was raised on the third day according to the Scriptures, and that he appeared to Cephas, then to the Twelve. Then he appeared to over five hundred brothers at one time; most of them are still alive, but some have fallen asleep. Then he appeared to James, then to all the apostles. Last of all, as to one abnormally born, he also appeared to me.*

This creed is considered to be one of the earliest sayings about Jesus.[115] It is also noteworthy that Paul mentions that many of the eyewitnesses themselves were still available.[116] Paul not only mentioned Jesus' brother, James, but he actually met James and Peter, two of Jesus' disciples.

I find it hard to believe that one could attribute an entire movement, historically grounded in Jewish historical roots and monotheism that emerged among polytheistic pagans, to a person who never actually walked the Earth. The mythicists must provide a coherent explanation of how Paul could have been punishing a movement for following a person who never existed—and then turn around and start a movement of the same "nonexistent" person. Since the mythicists seem to lack such an explanation, there is good reason to be skeptical of their claim that Jesus is entirely a myth.

The facts seem to make more probable the idea that there was a messianic claimant when Saul was a young man, and that he was charged to gather up and arrest people who followed that claimant and later was converted himself because he experienced seeing Jesus alive. Even if Paul had a hallucination of the resurrected Christ, it does not follow that Jesus was not a real person whom the Jewish Temple authorities were trying to punish out of existence.

Matthew, Mark, Luke, and John

The most thorough accounts about Jesus come from the gospel writers themselves. It is here that we find comprehensive and detailed information about the claims of Jesus as well as of His miracles. To have multiple accounts such as these demonstrates that there must have been a Jewish man named Jesus who existed in the first century, and that an event took place that prompted these narratives to be rapidly circulated. This does not, in and of itself, prove that every single claim in these gospel narratives is exactly as it happened; however, it does demonstrate that these narratives are valid sources that Jesus must have existed.

Chapter 22

A MYTH OF THE MYTH

"We do not err because truth is difficult to see. It is visible at a glance. We err because this is more comfortable."
Alexander Solzhenitsyn

I'm a skeptic, but I'm not a radical skeptic. I want to go where the evidence leads—and when it comes to Jesus' existence, there's little doubt. So why does the Jesus myth hypothesis exist? I suspect it is a presupposition towards philosophical naturalism, the belief that nothing outside the natural world such as gods, spirits, angels, demons, or any kind of miracles exist. All that remains for them, then, is to explain away the Christian movement as a whole. Bart Ehrman clarifies the mythicists' place in history:

> *It is fair to say that mythicists as a group, and as individuals, are not taken seriously by the vast majority of scholars in the field of New Testament, early Christianity, ancient history, and theology. . . . [T]he idea that Jesus did not exist is a modern notion. It has no ancient precedents. It was made up in the eighteenth century. One might as well call it a modern myth, the myth of the mythical Jesus.*[117]

One of the most influential Bible scholars of the 20th century, F.F. Bruce, adds, "Some writers may toy with the fancy of a 'Christ-myth,' but they do not do so on the ground of historical evidence. The historicity of Christ is as axiomatic for an unbiased historian as the historicity of Julius Caesar. It is not historians who propagate the 'Christ-myth' theories."[118]

Which Jesus?

Traveling overseas is exciting. I've seen new places, learned different customs, and watched various forms of performance media, all while making new friends. However, it is also exhausting to meet so many people, shake so many hands, and answer so many questions. By the end, all I desire is some quiet time alone, so that I can rest my mind and watch a movie.

While on a four-hour train ride through South Asia, I was in need of one of those quiet times. I plopped on my seat hoping to have the entire bench to myself. I fired up my laptop and put on my headphones—and then a man sat down next to me and started talking. It was unusual; in most foreign cultures, people are not talkative with strangers and keep to themselves.

"Hello. Are you American?" he asked. I nodded, and he quickly followed with, "Are you a Muslim?"

I wasn't expecting the question, though perhaps I should have; he was dressed in traditional Islamic garb for that culture. *Wow,* I thought. *Here I am on a mission trip to share my faith with university students, and now a Muslim is going to try to convert me. Cool!*

I pulled the headphones out of my ears. "I am not a Muslim," I replied. "I am a Christian."

"Why aren't you a Muslim?" he asked.

When I'd entered the train, all I wanted to do was get to my movie. But now I was being given an opportunity by the Lord to engage directly with a Muslim on the issues of life and faith. I silently prayed, *Okay, God. Let's do this.*

As we launched into our conversation, the man told me that Muslims believe in Jesus, but the difference is that they think Christians have changed the gospel stories to make Him more than a man. In other words, they believe the Jesus of evangelical

Christianity is *not* the Jesus of history. The evangelical version of Jesus, he said, is a myth developed over centuries that did originate with the actual Jesus that Muslims recognize.

It was not the first time I'd heard this view. Back in the 1980s a group of scholars met to renew the historical search for Jesus. As the group expanded with laymen and professionals from other fields, they became known as the Jesus Seminar.[119] They essentially made the same claim—the Jesus of Christian faith is not the real Jesus of history. In their meetings, they voted on which of Jesus' sayings and actions were more likely genuine and which were not. This less extreme perspective suggested that only portions of the traditional Christ are myth. For the Jesus Seminar, the myth was anything supernatural as well as Jesus' claims of divinity. For my new Muslim friend, the myth was that Jesus claimed to be divine and died on a Roman cross.

Think of their perspectives as similar to how we see Santa Claus. As a child, I had no idea that the character was originally and loosely based on a real fourth-century bishop. The almost cult-like veneration of this bishop, brought to North America as a Dutch tradition, was adapted over time to the personality we know today that rides in a sleigh and shimmies down chimneys (or, in the case of my Tucson home, entered through the sliding-glass door of our patio). Santa Claus is myth and legend developed over time and tradition, but based on a real human being.

So do the gospels of the New Testament (the books of Matthew, Mark, Luke, and John) simply present a Santa Claus version of Jesus, the real human being from Nazareth? Or do they present the genuine Jesus?

The New Testament Witness

Popular fiction and blogs can sometimes provide great historical information. They can also continue to propagate misunderstanding. As the saying goes, if you repeat something often enough, people will believe it. As I have toured the United

States over many years, I have come across the common belief that the New Testament is a conspiratorial collection of writings selected by a religious group of elites during the fourth century under the Roman Emperor Constantine.

Under a split empire, Constantine apparently had a vision of a flaming cross that would lead him to victory before a battle that he later won. As he united Rome, an edict was created to give freedom of religion to Christians, as well as other faiths. Constantine later convened a council of church leaders known as the Council of Nicea. According to popular fiction from authors such as Dan Brown in his *The DaVinci Code*, series, it was during this time that the New Testament books were *assembled* and the fiction of the divine Christ was born. Truths about Jesus were suppressed and a mythical version was spread.[120]

However, fiction is just that: fiction. The evidence reveals a very different story. When we examine the writings of the earliest students of the original disciples of Jesus (commonly known as the early church fathers) as well as the manuscript and archaeological evidence, we gain great confidence that the four gospels of the New Testament are early and accurate accounts of the life of Jesus. The stories in the gospels were either written by eyewitnesses themselves, or contained sayings and testimonies directly from eyewitnesses—Jesus' early followers and those who established the first Christian communities or churches.

The question is, how can we really trust that the early eyewitness accounts were passed on from person to person accurately before they were ever written down? The answer begins by historically understanding how these eyewitnesses were taught to learn stories and communicate them to others. Let's examine how the Bible as we know it today came in to existence.

Chapter 23

CAN WE TRUST THE BIBLE?

"I do not feel obliged to believe that the same God who has endowed us with sense, reason, and intellect has intended us to forgo their use."
Galileo Galilei

For over two decades, I have retained my knowledge of the smallest details of my illusions. Because I value performing the effects exactly as they were passed on to me and repeat or practice them as often as possible, it makes the execution of those details nearly perfect every time. I have also studied Wing Chun Kung Fu. My shīfu (master or teacher) was a student of Yip Man, the famed martial arts master and teacher of Bruce Lee. Much like the art of illusion, there was strong emphasis on getting each motion correct and knowing why every detail is important, so that we could preserve and honor the tradition of the art in its purest form.

Both illusion and martial arts are examples of the type of "passing on" of information practiced in the first century. The early Christians had a high regard for maintaining a pure form of the tradition and a high regard for repeating the information as often as possible.

Ancient Jewish memorization and oral tradition required accuracy.

First century Jewish children were required to memorize the first five books of the Hebrew scriptures called the Torah. Although many may not have had formal training in reading and writing like a scribe, a priest, or a government official, they would have been trained from a very young age the importance of passing on the stories of the Torah accurately, as they believed them to be the words of truth about God. The Hebrew scriptures even describe how they were to memorize the stories: to bind them to their foreheads, write them on their doorposts, and recite them day and night in order to accurately pass them down from generation to generation. In Jesus' day, His disciples viewed His teaching as coming from God and equal with scripture, and the New Testament epistles contain multiple references to this oral tradition. In short, they were well equipped to retain and retell the stories accurately.

In addition, life-altering experiences lend to memorability. The audiences responded to Jesus in the most profound ways due to His unique presentation style. He taught in word pictures called parables. Not only did these stories have a profound impact, but the deeds Jesus performed had a deep emotional impact on their lives. I may not be able to remember what I had for dinner last night or what interesting stories I read on Facebook, but I'll remember every word my wife said to me the night of our first kiss. Momentous or significant events make for better memories. Critics are mistaken to conclude, without evidence, that the first Christians offered unreliable testimony in light of the facts of Jewish oral traditions of the first century, the memorable fashion in which Jesus taught, and the transformative nature of what He taught and did.

The Gospels were written early.

The New Testament writings were originally written on a material created from a water plant called papyrus. When copies of the early gospels were made, scribes used papyrus because it was much less expensive than animal skins. Although papyrus does not last long in wet conditions, worn and damaged copies do exist today and are called manuscripts. A manuscript is a *copy* of an ancient piece of literature. New Testament manuscripts were discovered in places that would have required time and heavy circulation to reach. What this shows is that the early church was concerned with spreading its message as fast as possible to as many people as they could. As a result, the gospels were copied rapidly on papyrus, and manuscripts exist that comprise most of the New Testament dating back to around 100-150 years after the originals were written. A complete New Testament manuscript exists that dates to about 250 years after the originals were written.[121] It was *not* hundreds of years later during the Council of Nicea that the New Testament was allegedly *assembled*, as the DaVinci myth purports. Rather, the council simply reaffirmed what had already been established by the very first students of the disciples of Jesus.

In the dating of some of the oldest manuscripts, such as the "Magdalen manuscript" fragment of Matthew's gospel, some expert paleographers[122] have staked their careers on these manuscripts dating to within twenty years of the original authorship in the first century.[123] This is unheard of for any other writings from ancient history. It was also once believed that the gospel of John was written sometime in the late second century. If John's gospel was written that late, it weakens the view that John provides a more accurate account of the life of Jesus than other writings. However, a manuscript of the gospel of John known as the *John Rylands papyri* was discovered in 1934. It's a very small fragment and was once considered one of the oldest manuscripts in existence, dating as early as the 90 A.D. and no later than 150 A.D. Since most scholars now believe that John penned the gospel of John in the first decade of that sixty year range, New Testament professor Dan Wallace makes the surprising remark that "it's possible, then, that this manuscript. . . was a copy of John's gospel when the ink was barely dry on the original document."[124]

In addition, none of the writers of Matthew, Mark, Luke, or John mention the destruction of the Jewish temple in Jerusalem in 70 A.D. This was a crucial event since Jesus Himself predicted the temple's destruction.[125] Certainly, any devout follower would have taken advantage of that level of proof and included it in the narrative if it had been written after 70 A.D.

The Gospels are eyewitness accounts.

Outside of the actual words of the New Testament, we first have the students of the original eyewitness followers of Jesus, also referred to as the early church fathers. Along with their pupils, these fathers affirmed in their writings that the New Testament gospels were eyewitness accounts. That would be like my great grandpa telling me war stories. These early church leaders lived several centuries before the first councils formalized the official New Testament collection (also known as the canon) that we know today in the Bible.

Not only do we have that external evidence of an early date of these gospels, we have within the gospels themselves evidence of being eyewitness accounts, not stories told much later by people who weren't there. For example, the gospel of John is written as an actual eyewitness account of Jesus. Words like *testify, testimony,* or *to witness* translated from the original language (mostly Greek) appear in John's gospel over forty times, almost double the amount of the remaining three gospels combined. The gospel also begins and ends with eyewitness testimony from the perspective of two witnesses. The first witness is John the Baptist; the second witness is the author, the disciple John.[126]

The gospel of Luke begins by stating that it is a narrative written from eyewitnesses who spoke directly to the author. "Many have undertaken to compile a narrative about the events that have been fulfilled among us, just as the original eyewitnesses and servants of the word handed them down to us. It also seemed good to me, since I have carefully investigated everything from the very first, to write to you in an orderly sequence." (Luke 1:1-4)

In his book, *Cold Case Christianity*, detective J. Warner Wallace points out several lines of evidence that the gospel of Mark was an account taken from the disciple Peter's perspective.[127] The detective points out that from the biblical passages we can confirm a relationship between Mark and Peter. Mark's gospel describes Peter with a unique familiarity, and Peter is mentioned most often. In addition, irrelevant information that would have been firsthand knowledge by Peter was included, while equally irrelevant facts (facts not relevant to the message or events of Jesus' life) that would have been an embarrassment to Peter as a church leader were left out. We also have, according to the early church fathers, several traditions that Mark wrote Peter's memoir and compiled his gospel based on the preaching of Peter.

The Gospels are profoundly preserved.

I explained to my Muslim friend on the train that the New Testament is the single most manuscript-rich assembly of writings in existence. In fact, not a single original manuscript of *any* literary work from the classic Roman and Greek periods exists today. All that we have are copies of copies of copies of the originals. Yet when I was in school and required to read Homer, Plato, and Aristotle, I was told that I was reading a publication of the original text. Therefore, I assumed these writings were locked away somewhere for safe keeping. That's not the case at all.

There are two notable features of nearly all works of antiquity: first, that the manuscripts are scarce; second, there is a significant gap in time from the original date of writing to the date of the first copy. More often than not, there are only a handful of copies that are hundreds and sometimes over one thousand years removed from the original. We have no idea what errors might have been made during those centuries of copying.

My Muslim train companion, however, was insistent. "The *Injeel* has been changed!" he exclaimed. The *Injeel* is the Islamic term that refers to the New Testament gospels. I popped open my laptop and showed him a timeline of every century since the second century that possessed manuscript copies of the New Testament gospels. In the original Greek language, there are currently over 5,800 New Testament gospel manuscripts in existence.[128] There are also 20,000 manuscripts of the New Testament translated into other languages dating from the late second to the fifteenth century. These do show copy errors and variants, I told him, but scholars have identified these mistakes because there are so many manuscripts to compare. Yet none of these errors have any significant bearing on the meaning of the text or essential beliefs about Jesus. Of the 25,000 lines in the New Testament gospels, only about forty are in question.

It's no wonder why Dr. Daniel B. Wallace states that there is not a single ancient literary work in existence that even comes close to this "embarrassment of riches."[129] "The variant readings about which any doubt remains among textual critics of the New Testament affect no material question of historic fact, or of Christian faith and practice," adds F.F. Bruce. "The evidence for our New Testament writings is ever so much greater than the evidence for many writings of classical authors, the authenticity of which no one dreams of questioning. And if the New Testament were a collection of secular writings, their authenticity would generally be regarded as beyond all doubt."[130]

In our discourse, my Muslim friend had an opposing response for every comment I made, but they were not rebuttals. He simply stated his theological views. He was intelligent, and he knew how to communicate the details of his beliefs. But after I showed him the data about whether or not the *Injeel* had been changed, he was silent. As I pointed to my graphs showing manuscript evidence of the four New Testament gospels from every century from the first to the invention of the printing press in the fifteenth century, where copying mistakes would no longer occur, I asked him, "If the Ineel has been changed, point to me when in history was it changed?" He simply let out a deep breath. "Hmmm," he pondered. "You've given me a lot to think about." We talked the entire four hour trip. He was polite and thanked me for my time. Then he gave me his business card. He was a professor at a university in Saudi Arabia. Who knows? Maybe the information I shared reshaped his thinking about whether or not the eyewitness accounts of Jesus' life have been changed.

The Gospels are historically reliable.

A couple of years ago I had the opportunity to travel to Israel. It was a fascinating excursion. Although I had read about many of the amazing archeological discoveries confirming the validity of the New Testament gospel accounts, it was great to see them firsthand. After all, if we are going to rely on Matthew, Mark, Luke, and John as eyewitness accounts to unmask the real Jesus, it's important that they demonstrate historical reliability.

As one of my mentors, Dr. Don Bierle, often said, "Whenever in doubt, just grab a shovel and head over to Israel. You'll find what you're looking for." Nearly every city, person, or major event in the Bible that has come into question has been found to be factual through the archeological evidence. This is particularly important when the New Testament writers mention a place with specific details that only an eyewitness would know about but that was never mentioned by any other historian of the time. For example, two pools mentioned in the book of John with geographic details (Bethesda and Siloam, both associated with miracles performed by Jesus) have been confirmed in archeological digs.[131]

The gospel writers also mention people that have no other historic references to their existence. Pontius Pilate and the Jewish high priest Joseph Caiaphas are both mentioned in the New Testament and nowhere else. Yet archeology has confirmed Pilate as being a real person through coins that were minted in his honor, as well as through an inscription of his name in Caesarea.[132] During road construction, a tractor fell into an ancient gravesite where Caiaphas' ossuary, a first century stone burial box with the deceased's name inscribed on it, was found.

Sometimes details are mentioned in the gospel narratives that do not relate to a person or a place but an object. One example of this is nails. Skeptics claimed in the 1970s that the New

Testament gospel writers were essentially fabricating decades or even hundreds of years later their references to Jesus being nailed to a cross. Nails, they said, were not used in crucifixion until the late second century at the earliest. When I was in Jerusalem, I saw the remains of a crucifixion victim's foot behind a glass box on display at a museum. Stuck to his ankle bone was a large nail. It was clear the nail had hit a knot in the wood and bent inward as he was being nailed to the cross. Apparently, the executioners chopped his ankle off and threw it into the bone box. The bone was dated to about 42 A.D. Nails were used for crucifixion during the time of Jesus.

From Myth to Magician

In the New Testament gospel writings, there are multiple early eyewitness accounts of the life of Jesus. The manuscript evidence shows that these accounts were preserved throughout time with a vast mountain of examinable manuscripts from every century since the lives of the first students of the disciples. These accounts demonstrate historical accuracy with minute details not possible had the stories been made up a long time later by Christians living in different regions. As I set out to do, I examined the writings of the earliest students of the original disciples of Jesus and completed my study with great confidence that the four gospels of the New Testament are early and accurate accounts either written by eyewitnesses themselves or containing sayings and testimonies directly from eyewitnesses of the life of Jesus. I am completely confident that we can, indeed, trust the accuracy of the Bible we have today. Is that enough? No.

Now that we have a trustworthy account, we can examine Christ's works and see, just as if we were there with the eyewitnesses, what He did and examine His miracles from the point of view of a magician to test whether Jesus was merely a clever magician—or something much more.

Chapter 24

Jesus: First Century Conjuror?

"What the eyes see and the ears hear, the mind believes."
Harry Houdini

When you're a kid, being a magician seems like a pretty innocent adventure. You go to the magic shop, pick up a couple beginners' effects, and then get ten dollars from your neighbor to perform for their five-year-old's birthday party.

Little did I know the amount of controversy that would come later after becoming a *Christian* illusionist. It seemed that after every performance, a well-meaning Christian accused me of utilizing a tool of evil, or "demon magic" as some of them labeled it. I was often directed to the Bible for example after example of how the devil used his power and influence to endow men and women with a chance to attain magical powers.

A common proof given as evidence of these powers is the magicians of Egypt in the book of Exodus. As we've seen from Section Two of this book, these attempts to outperform Moses were futile, since the magicians of Pharaoh's court were using deception and trickery, pretending that their effects were real.

A team of magicians and I decided to illustrate this interpretation by developing an illusion not very different than what those magicians did ages ago. I'll admit it was a bit controversial, but the startling reaction from the audience was too priceless to pass up. I walked out into the audience holding a cane. I tapped it on the auditorium floor and, right there in the middle of the audience, the cane instantly transformed into a living snake in my hands. Many people screamed, and some even raced out of the auditorium doors. I then explained that what I did was sleight of hand and said, "There is no such thing as real magic."

I was trying to illustrate just how easy it was to create the illusion of a miracle. Naturally, the next question is, "If I could duplicate a biblical miracle such as turning a stick into a snake, can we not explain away all of the miracles of the Bible as mere trickery?" More specifically, could Jesus have been using trickery and deception—that is, *natural means*—to accomplish His miracles?

Historical Context

Before we look at some of the effects that the New Testament gospel eyewitnesses saw Jesus perform, the effects those witnesses genuinely believed were supernatural miracles, we need to put things into context.[133] While researching for this chapter, I came across a YouTube video posted by a self-proclaimed atheist.[134] He showed several magicians performing tricks such as bodily vanishing and walking on water, faith healing, and changing liquids into different kinds of beverages. His point was simple: these magicians did exactly what Jesus did. What this YouTube post failed to clarify was that, to pull off these tricks, these illusionists often required a tremendous amount of equipment, advanced technology, a modern understanding of chemistry, and a good amount of funds.

When touring in San Antonio, Texas as a nineteen year old, I was with André Kole and a few other members of our team one night in a boat on the canal along that city's famous River Walk. As I stared at the reflection of the lights sparkling in the dark water, an idea occurred to me of how to create the illusion of walking on water. I asked André Kole if there was a way to create the illusion of walking on a natural body of water such as a lake. Kole had already performed live on stage the illusion of standing on water in a tank. "It's impossible," he replied. Then I shared my method of accomplishing the illusion. After my lengthy explanation, he simply smiled and said, "Interesting." Had I actually created my method of walking across a natural body of water at that time, it would have cost me tens of thousands of dollars–which I didn't have as a nineteen-year-old kid (and, incidentally, still don't).

In addition, my method required ideas and knowledge of technology and science that did not exist in the first century when Jesus lived. He was limited to the knowledge, science, and technology of His day. Jesus did not have a home, much less an income. It is terribly misguided to point to modern magic performances as an example of how Jesus might have been a magician. From the point of view of an expert illusionist, Jesus could not possibly have faked things like walking on water, multiplying food, or healing the sick when limited to the funds and technology available to Him.

Multiplying the Loaves and Fish

During my stage act, I had a seven-minute routine where I'd make nine white doves and a blue and gold macaw appear from my bare hands. Using the concepts I learned as a magician to make animals seemingly appear out of thin air, I tried to picture Jesus using similar and necessary techniques of the art of illusion to accomplish miracles such as His feeding of the masses, the only miracle Jesus performed (besides His own resurrection) that is recorded by all four New Testament gospels. I have identified four critical observations that undermine the possibility that Jesus could have used some form of trickery to feed such a large crowd of people.

He was in the wilderness. Jesus instructed that He and His disciples should withdraw from the crowds by boat, traveling around the Sea of Galilee to a remote a place in the wilderness. Having been to the Sea of Galilee, it's easy to picture the crowds running and following Him in order to arrive at the shoreline before Jesus and His disciples disembarked. The Sea of Galilee is a large freshwater lake in Israel that's about thirteen miles long and just over eight miles wide. It's big, but not too big to accurately fit the description of "sea." Although the crowds were unrelenting in their pursuit of Jesus, He felt compassion for them and resumed healing the sick once they returned to shore. Jesus also spent a great deal of time teaching the crowds.

When I saw famous magicians Siegfried and Roy make an elephant appear on stage, I knew this was only possible to do in a strictly controlled environment. It was not an illusion they could perform effectively just anywhere. Even when a magician makes something as grand as a car or an airplane appear outdoors, the magician must have control of the environment. The fact that Jesus and His disciples went to a remote place in the wilderness makes it highly difficult to *hide* enough food for such a big crowd. There was no way Jesus could've controlled His environment as a magician would.

The disciples had no part in making the food appear. In fact, the disciples wanted Jesus to send everyone away so they could go back to their villages to eat. As amazing as it was to hear Jesus' profound teaching and witness people being healed of their sicknesses, those who had gathered were surely getting weary and hungry. The disciples recognized this and saw it as a good excuse to disburse the crowd. Had the disciples been privy to a grand illusion plan from Jesus, they would've made no such request. Nor would they have unrealistically offered to buy food for such a large gathering of people. Yet when they handed out a few loaves and fishes, Scripture says everyone ate their fill.

As a magician, not only do you need control of your environment to execute an illusion, you need help! The greater the level of sophistication and magnitude of the effect, the more *stooges* a magician needs. It's nearly impossible to predict the behavior of other people when putting on an act. And even then, things can still fail miserably. One evening when I was working on a cruise ship, I wanted to do an effect where I seemed to magically appear out of nowhere in the middle of the audience. One of my assistants failed to ensure that the right item was set in precisely the right way at exactly the right moment. The music rose, the spotlights glared on the spot where I was to appear, and—well, I wasn't there. Let's just say I was detained.

Though I was embarrassed, I finally did come running several minutes later from the back of the audience. The cruise director commented, "Well, he's a magician—and magicians sometimes disappear. We hope you've enjoyed the show!" Even the false godman Baba had the aid of his security team in making small, easy-to-hide pieces of jewelry appear. Baba was the only person I've seen in my lifetime who was able to use trickery to give things to a group of people, but he never made enough necklaces appear to give to over ten thousand people in one afternoon.

The crowd was massive. The eyewitness accounts in the Bible estimated the crowd to be about 5,000 men, not including women and children. It's safe to say that there were probably 7,000 to 12,000 mouths to feed. When any magician sets out to perform, the size of the audience determines what can be done. If there is no way to estimate in advance how many people will attend the show, it's nearly impossible to come fully prepared without bringing your entire repertoire. Jesus would have had to estimate precisely how many people could have shown up that day. It's conceivable to manufacture a way to feed a few dozen people in much the same way I can make a few birds appear. But to feed thousands? There's no way a magician can do it, especially in the middle of the wilderness.

The lack of available resources. This was illustrated by Philip's reaction when he tried to calculate what it would cost to meet Jesus' request to feed everyone. He made the comment that even with two hundred denarii, which I estimated to be around five to eight thousand dollars today, it would still not come close to feeding so many with anything more than a pinch per person. Collectively, Jesus and the disciples didn't have enough money to literally feed these people, much less create an elaborate illusion of feeding them.

In actuality, the New Testament texts strongly infer that Jesus intended to perform the supernatural feeding of the throng all along; He was simply using his inquiries to test His disciples' faith in Him and teach them a lesson in trusting God. More often than not, the disciples limited themselves to natural ways to see the world, even as Jesus' ministry unfolded. Again, the disciples' response is relevant because it shows they were not aware or expectant of His plan to perform a miracle.

To their astonishment, Jesus blessed and broke the bread and divided up the fish. He passed them to the disciples, and they in turn passed them out to the crowds who were likely seated in groups of fifty to one hundred. This went on until everyone ate *and was filled.* When finished, there were up to twelve baskets of leftover pieces of bread and fish.

In the end, this was and is impossible for a magician to achieve. By Himself, Jesus fed a huge group of people in a remote location without aid, using only supernatural means. There is no other explanation.

Walking on Water

It was after this incredible mass feeding that Jesus again instructed His disciples to push off onto the Sea of Galilee in a boat, but this time without Him. As was His habit, He retreated to the hills to pray throughout the evening. Matthew 14:23-27 records what happened next:

> *. . . the boat was already over a mile from land, battered by the waves, because the wind was against them. Around three in the morning, He came toward them walking on the sea. When the disciples saw Him walking on the sea, they were terrified. "It's a ghost!" they said, and cried out in fear. Immediately Jesus spoke to them. "Have courage! It is I. Don't be afraid." (Matthew 14:23-27 Holman Christian Standard Bible)*

I remember the first time I saw David Copperfield fly across the stage like Peter Pan. I knew that it wasn't easy, even for a seasoned professional like him. I also knew it was expensive and required advanced technology—as do any illusions of a grand scale.

About ten or so years after that night on the San Antonio Riverwalk where I shared my vision with André Kole for creating a "walk on water" illusion, André became the first person to ever achieve the illusion of walking across a natural body of water. The effect was filmed on Saguaro Lake near Phoenix, Arizona by the BBC and later aired on a Discovery Channel special on the miracles of Jesus. In the program, André was careful to point out that the illusion was accomplished entirely by natural means. Sometimes I like to think that our boat ride in San Antonio inspired him. I recall being with André as he fielded phone calls from some of the world's best magicians asking permission to perform his effect of walking on water. Since then, many have copied his effect, with minor variations, to accomplish the stunning illusion. Magic is a secret art!

If I could, as a nineteen year old, come up with a method of walking on water through trickery, and since André Kole and others have done the illusion since then, is that alone enough to prove that Jesus used trickery to walk on the Sea of Galilee to His disciples? I tried to take my advanced understanding of how illusions are performed and simplify them to their most basic concepts without requiring advanced technology; the basic secret of the illusion stripped of all of its modernity and dropped into a first century context.

As with the feeding of the crowds, Jesus needed to predict exactly where the boat would be at three in the morning, and He would have needed a lot of help. The New Testament accounts indicate He had no assistants and had a general, but not precise measure of where the boat was located. In addition, He required control of the immediate environment. But at the time of the event, a storm was raging over the waters. At its maximum depth, the Sea of Galilee is over 140 feet deep. In those circumstances, it's inconceivable to develop a means to pull off the illusion. Kole's effect on a much smaller lake in Arizona, minus the darkness and the storm, cost thousands of dollars, months of planning, and large amounts of equipment.

But perhaps Jesus wasn't actually walking on the water, anyway. Could the eyewitnesses have experienced an optical illusion or mirage? Perhaps Jesus was simply walking in shallow water that, from a distance, appeared to be the sea.

The magician Dynamo, once attempted to perform walking on water on the river Thames.[135] He created a platform that, from a distance, made it look as though he were walking on the river's surface. In the video of his effect, viewers can observe that his feet are semi-submerged and not standing *on* the water. What was tragic for Dynamo, though, was the release of the unedited video that showed his boat accidentally ram the platform he was walking upon.[136] Oops.

The New Testament account, though, makes clear that even in the unlikely event that Jesus created a platform near a shallow edge of the Sea of Galilee, He walked out into the middle of the lake. No platform or other apparatus is possible at those depths. Plus, He wasn't alone on the water's surface. The story shares that the disciple Peter asked to walk out to Jesus and did, at least for a short distance. Fear of the storm caused him to begin to sink, the account states, and Jesus had to catch hold of Peter without sinking Himself. Again, there was no natural means by which this could be achieved.

It's the end of the account, though, that is most significant. When Jesus got into the boat, the storm ceased. The only logical conclusion is that Jesus walked on the water, hauled someone out of the water, and quieted the weather through supernatural means. No magician's trick could do these things.

Healing the Sick

Of course, Jesus was most known for healing the sick. He did so on an almost constant basis throughout His final years on the Earth. In this modern day, the concept of faith healing is nothing new. People all over the world claim to heal the sick. I remember watching a television special that exposed the antics of many popular televangelists and their claims of miracle healings. They duped their viewing audiences into requesting special healing objects such as prayer cloths, holy water, or any other "blessed" item these charlatans could come up with—in return for a significant donation. Yet I never saw any of these men or women perform a healing that had clear visual evidence.

There are others, called psychic surgeons, who looked more convincing. Years ago, I was invited by one of the largest mission organizations in the world to travel to South Asia to appear at a press conference and visit several medical universities to promote my tour and demonstrate and explain how psychic surgery was performed. Sadly, a man at that time was performing this effect and gaining notoriety with celebrities and government officials, many of whom claimed to have experienced healing at his services.

Psychic Surgery

Psychic surgery is the claimed ability to perform a healing procedure by physically removing a disease without making any kind of incision on the patient. A psychic surgeon performs this feat with his bare hands and removes the patients' illnesses without using any tools or leaving behind any scars. When observed, it does seem that the surgeon is literally reaching into the body and removing what appears to be bloody tissue. It's pretty gory. This tissue, it was claimed, was the disease being taken out. The patient then rose from his table, cleaned up with a bowl of water and a towel, and walked away. Talk about your "outpatient" surgery.

Yet I knew that these psychic surgeons did was really nothing more than *very* simple sleight of hand to create the illusion of pulling out bloody tissue from a person's abdomen. In demonstrating the effect in South Asia, I not only pulled the diseased bloody "tissue" out of my volunteer in exactly the same manner as the supposed psychic surgeon, I also removed a rubber chicken that had apparently left behind an egg. It's fakery of the most basic kind.

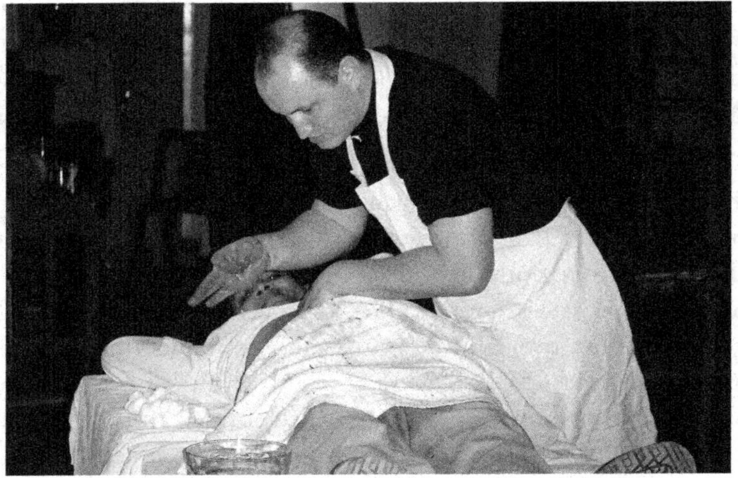

Adrian Van Vactor debunking psychic surgery in a country in South Asia

So how do these people, then, claim to have been healed? What about those who claim to have been healed by supposed faith healers also using deception to convince their audience they have the gift of healing?

Organic vs. Functional Illness

A functional disorder, illness, or disease is one in which "there is an abnormal change in the function of an organ, but no structural alteration in the tissues involved."[137] For most people, something going on in their body that prompts them to schedule a visit to the doctor is usually functional in nature. There is no associated organic or pathological change in tissue that can be detected either directly or by some sort of scan and lab. Functional symptoms are things like abdominal and back pain, indigestion, headaches, and allergies.

An organic illness, on the other hand, includes blindness, broken bones, arthritis, or cancer. It is a disease in which there is a structural alteration to organs or tissue.[138] Psychic surgeons and faith healers never "heal" organic illnesses—only functional illnesses. People who experience feelings of healing in these cases, therefore, are not feeling the effects of an actual healing, but are instead experiencing a psychosomatic response or placebo effect. There is no organic change in their bodies; instead, their positive, even faith-inspired thought, can often bring temporary relief from functional symptoms. But no real diseases are actually healed.

The term "placebo" is common in reference in drug trials. It's a remarkable phenomenon in which a placebo—a *fake treatment*, an inactive substance like sugar, distilled water, or saline solution—can sometimes improve a patient's condition simply because the person has the expectation that it will be helpful.[139] In drug trials, one part of the test group is given the actual drug, while the other part is given the placebo. Both groups are led to believe that they are taking the drug. A psychosomatic response—*psyche* meaning mind, and *soma* meaning body—can also be enhanced if the healing looks believable, as was the case with the psychic healers and their fake blood and tissue.[140] The physical sleight of hand further increased the potential of the patient's response to be positive.

Yet when cataloging the healing miracles Jesus performed, He *only* healed organic illnesses. Jesus never relied on placebos or psychosomatic symptoms. In one New Testament gospel eyewitness case, for example, Jesus healed a man born blind. He upset the religious leaders because He did the miracle on the Sabbath, the day when Jews were not allowed to do any work. These religious authorities went to the man's parents to verify that the man was, in fact, born blind. As the leaders continued to try to get the man to admit that Jesus had sinned for healing on the Sabbath, the man responded, "Whether or not he's a sinner, I don't know. One thing I do know: I was blind, and now I can see!"

From Magician to Messiah?

During a television broadcast, David Copperfield said:

> *The miracles of the Bible go beyond anything that any magician or illusionist could ever perform. . . but greater than any physical miracle was the ability of a man named Jesus to bring purpose and meaning to the lives of millions of people throughout the centuries.*

I was satisfied that the miracles Jesus accomplished could not be explained by natural means. Up to this point in my training as an illusionist, I had become an increasingly proud skeptic. I found myself walking dangerously close to presuming that the supernatural was not possible, period. Now, I could no longer hold on to that skepticism. As tempting as it was to end my quest, I pressed on, determined to let the evidence be my teacher.

Where had the evidence led me so far? I discovered that my new found faith was not placed in a mythical character, but a person, Jesus Christ, who truly existed in history. I also discovered that the men and women who walked and talked with Jesus accurately passed on and even tested for themselves the events they experienced. Finally, my examination of the miracles of Jesus within the context of the very field I was most acquainted with, the art of deception, made the argument that Jesus was merely a first century magician the most preposterous idea of all. Jesus actually performed deeds using supernatural means—He was not a magician, nor an illusionist.

So then, who was Jesus? If not a myth and not a magician, who... what? The stage was set for the next phase of my quest – to examine what Jesus actually said about Himself and why His followers came to believe that He was the Messiah, the anticipated coming Jewish King and divine Son of God.

Chapter 25

THE SAVIOR UNMASKED

"I am a Jew, but I am enthralled by the luminous figure of the Nazarene. . . . His personality pulsates in every word. No myth is filled with such life."

Albert Einstein
The Saturday Evening Post, October 26, 1929

When I was about sixteen years old, I was on the phone with my friend, Allan, when he told me that he had something very profound to share with me.

"Adrian, Jesus is God. Not just a son of God, but God."

I didn't know what to think. For the next hour, with my new Bible in hand, we went through various sayings of Jesus where He clearly made divine claims.

I remember listening to another one of my mentors, Dr. Don Bierle, give an analogy of what your neighbor or friend might think if you were to go up to him one day and simply say, "I am from above. You are from below." As Bierle pointed out, they might be pretty confused or think you've simply lost your marbles.

When Jesus began His short earthly ministry, He made a quick and tremendous impact through many miracles and acts of love, acceptance, and charity. What brought Him trouble were the words He said.[141] The more people listened, the more they began to react, much as I did to my friend's assertion on the phone. "Did he just say what I think he said?"

Jesus claimed to be the Messiah.

When John the Baptist was imprisoned for preaching publicly that King Herod's marriage to his brother's wife was immoral, he sent some of his disciples to go and ask Jesus personally and plainly if He was the Messiah.[142] The following was Jesus' response, as reported in the Gospels of Matthew 11 and Luke 7.

> *Go and report to John what you hear and see: the blind see, the lame walk, those with skin diseases are healed, the deaf hear, the dead are raised, and the poor are told the good news. And if anyone is not offended because of me, he is blessed.*

Why didn't Jesus simply say "yes"? A careful look into His sayings about a valid testimony reveal that Jesus knew, according to Jewish law and culture, that His own word, or any one man's word, was not sufficient evidence for any testimony. A "yes" answer would only mean *Jesus* believed He was the Messiah. Jesus expresses this sentiment clearly in John's gospel account when He says: "If I testify about myself, my testimony is not valid. There is another who testifies about me, and I know that the testimony he gives about me is valid. You have sent messengers to John, and he has testified to the truth. . . . But I have a greater testimony than John's because of the works that the Father has given me to accomplish. These very works I am doing testify about me that the Father has sent me." (John 5:31-36)

Jesus went directly to the evidence by repeating a commonly believed saying or understanding about the Messiah and the things that would surround His coming. During another account, Jesus and His followers were cornered by an eager group of His fellow Jews, who pressed Jesus in order to make it clear to everyone that He did, indeed, claim to be the Messiah. In this account, Jesus had departed from teaching in the temple and was teaching just outside of it during a religious festival. He proclaimed that God was His Father and had given Him authority to lay His life down, bring it back up again, and then give eternal life to His followers. The angry crowd asked, "How long are you going to keep us in suspense? If you are the Messiah, tell us plainly." Jesus replied, "I did tell you and you don't believe. . . . The works that I do in my Father's name testify about me. But you don't believe because you are not my sheep" (John 10:25-26).

Jesus had repeatedly performed miracles that critics and skeptics could not explain. Since these signs and deeds were commonly understood to accompany the coming Messiah, Jesus knew that it was not His lack of clarity that confused His critics but rather their lack of faith in their own Scriptures. Here, Jesus not only makes it abundantly clear that He is the Messiah, He adds insult to injury by suggesting that His critics are not God's sheep, and that the real sheep are given by God to the real Shepherd, Jesus, who gives eternal life to them.

Their reaction was blunt:

> *Again his Jewish opponents picked up stones to stone him, but Jesus said to them, "I have shown you many good works from the Father. For which of these do you stone me?"*
>
> *"We are not stoning you for any good work," they replied, "but for blasphemy, because you, a mere man, claim to be God.*
>
> (John 10:31-33)

Jesus claimed to be the Son of God.

In Mark 12, Jesus shared a parable in which He described a vineyard owner, his son, his servants, and some farmers. In it, the vineyard owner leases out his land to a group of farmers. After some time, the owner sent his servant to go and collect the owner's cut. However, the farmers beat the servant and sent him away empty handed. This occurred several more times; a few servants were even killed. As a last resort, the landowner reasoned that if he sent his only son, the farmers would respect him and fulfill their contract. Instead, the farmers kill the son, reasoning to themselves that if the owner's only heir is dead, they'd be able to keep the land for themselves.

The identification of each character in the parable is this: the landowner was God, the land is the Promised Land of Israel, the farmers were the Israelites, and the servants were the Old Testament prophets who communicated to the Israelites on God's behalf. Jesus then implied that He was the son and heir symbolized in the story. The way in which the religious leaders listening to the parable responded was very telling. They knew Jesus was referring to Himself as this heir who was essentially equal with the owner, God, over and above all of the previous generations of prophets and the rest of the Israelites. The religious authorities wanted to arrest him at that moment, but were afraid of the crowd's response.

Jesus repeatedly referred to Himself as the one and only Son of God, but that wasn't all that He claimed. In John 5, after healing the blind man on the Sabbath, Jesus referred to Himself as "the Son" multiple times. He further claimed that His Father, God, had given all judgment to Him to give eternal life to anyone He chose. When the authorities challenged Jesus for working on the Sabbath, Jesus said that God, His Father, was still working, and so He would still be working. Jesus was not referring to resting from the labor of one's vocations, the original intent of the Sabbath, but that He and His Father were at work changing the lives and hearts of the people. The text went on to highlight how His words were perceived. "This is why the Jews began trying all the more to kill him: Not only was he breaking the Sabbath, but he was even calling God his own father, making himself equal with God." (John 5:18)

Jesus claimed to be the Son of Man.

Jesus often referred to Himself as the Son of Man, a title not attributed to Jesus by the early church and only used once in the book of Acts, the biblical account of the events of the very first Christians after Jesus' resurrection. Jesus used this phrase to refer to Himself no less than eighty two times in the New Testament gospels and more than any other self-descriptive title in His speeches or parables.

It's interesting that Jesus used the definite article "*the.*" Instead of saying *a* son of man, He is *the* Son of Man. The phrase originates from the Old Testament book of Daniel where the prophet tells of the coming of a king personified as the nation of Israel. This coming king, the Son of Man, would be given all authority and glory, a kingdom, and an eternal reign over the entire world. By using that definite article, Jesus pointed to this figure referenced in Daniel, distinguishing it from other similar uses of the phrase in the Hebrew Bible.[143]

Jewish trial confirms His claims.

In one of the earliest eyewitness accounts of Jesus in Mark 14, the author records an event where Jesus is brought before the Sanhedrin soon after His arrest. The Sanhedrin was a court of Jewish leadership consisting of roughly seventy priests and scribes, and each of the gospels tells us this group wanted to condemn Jesus to death. These religious judges decided matters of Jewish law, but they were still under Roman rule. Rome gave the Jews limited authority to deal with matters of their own religious practices, so long as they did not interfere with Roman law or communal peace.

By this time, the Jewish authorities had leveled official charges against Jesus in an attempt to cause Him to commit blasphemy in front of their high court. In Mark 14:61-62 they press further:

> *Again the high priest asked him, "Are you the Messiah, the Son of the Blessed One?"*
>
> *"I am," said Jesus. "And you will see the Son of Man sitting at the right hand of the Mighty One and coming on the clouds of heaven."*

Their question contained two of the three primary claims about Jesus: that He was the Messiah and the Son of God. In His answer, Jesus added the third, *the Son of Man.*

The high priest immediately tore his robes and declared, "Why do we still need witnesses? You have heard the blasphemy! What is your decision?"[144] The high court condemned Jesus and had Him beaten repeatedly before turning Him over to the Roman authorities for another trial before the governor of Judea, Pontius Pilate. Interestingly, Pilate saw no reason to execute Jesus; the fact that it was Pilate's final decision to do so shows that Jesus was not considered to be a common criminal being crucified for breaking a serious Roman law. From a Roman perspective, Jesus was a Jewish problem thrust into the hands of Pilate, who had him crucified to keep the peace.

"Christ in front of Pilate" by Mihály Munkácsy (1844-1900)[159]

There are many other instances where Jesus' actions and words pointed to His divine nature. His arrest and conviction by the angry Jewish leaders indicate they perceived Jesus as having made these claims to divinity. Since the Jewish religious authorities accused Jesus of blasphemy, they demanded that He be handed over to the Romans for crucifixion, since Jews were not allowed to crucify individuals under Roman law. Upon His execution, the Roman soldiers posted a sign on His cross:

Jesus the Nazarene
The King of the Jews[145]

Since Jesus was considered by them to be a messianic phony, it's not surprising to see this mockery. What is surprising, though, is the wording they used. No follower of Jesus ever called Him "King of the Jews". This was never used as a title for Jesus by the early church fathers or later in the early church itself. This demonstrates the common perception among the Romans of Jesus' claims about Himself.

My friend Allan was right about one thing; Jesus certainly claimed to be God, even though the cost of such a claim would be certain death. But what about His death? What about the claims of His resurrection? From the point of view of a magician, I could understand a person ignoring the miracles Jesus performed if He simply died then faded away into history. However, the ultimate proof of His claims—and the bedrock of the Christian faith—took place after His crucifixion. Was Jesus' resurrection an elaborate deception, or the ultimate miracle proving His claims?

Chapter 26

THE RESURRECTION: MAGIC OR MIRACLE?

"If Jesus rose from the dead, then you have to accept all that he said; if he didn't rise from the dead, then why worry about any of what he said? The issue on which everything hangs is not whether or not you like his teaching but whether or not he rose from the dead."

Timothy J. Keller

One thing my wife always makes fun of me for is my inability to handle pungent smells. It's her job to take out the trash, unless she's interested in a good laugh. You can find some very humorous videos online of fathers losing control as they change their baby's diapers. I guess that's what makes me a great cook: my insanely great sense of smell.

During one of my more recent tours, we were in a small village in Bulgaria. We began to set up and draw a crowd for our performance, when suddenly someone asked us to move to a different area, for the community was about to enter into mourning. We didn't fully understand what they were mourning, until we began to make our way through the village to gather more "intel."

We approached a home where several were gathered, and our translator was able to surmise what had happened. An elderly woman was found deceased in her home and had been undiscovered for several days. We realized that insisting on doing a program right then and there would be terribly inconsiderate, so we began to make our way back to our van. It was then that I experienced the true smell of human death. I didn't see a body, but I didn't need to. I've smelled dead animals before, but my keen nose was not at all prepared for the scent I was about to experience. Death was literally in the air, and so powerful that I immediately went into uncontrollable retching

I can't begin to imagine what the disciples experienced when they saw their anticipated king get arrested, beaten, and executed. The following four facts are relatively accepted by all Jesus scholars today.

Fact 1: Certain death

No one ever expected Jesus to die, except Jesus.[146] If Jesus was merely a magician performing magic effects similar to what modern day magicians like I perform, His death would have been a very unexpected outcome for Him. And even though He consistently predicted this outcome, Jesus' followers never really accepted what would later become a very certain fact of the historical eyewitness record.[147]

One of the hallmarks of the genuineness of the gospel narratives is the imperfect ways in which they end. For example, right up until Jesus' arrest, His followers had a preconceived notion of what the Messiah was going to do, and Jesus had met and exceeded those expectations. The disciples' common belief was that the Messiah, a kingly descendant of David, was going to overthrow their oppressors and restore the Davidic throne as the final, good king they had long awaited. When the temple priests arrived with soldiers to arrest Jesus, Peter grabbed a sword and sliced the ear off of one of the temple servants, a reaction to an unexpected event that was very much in character for Peter. An arrest, seeing their Messiah in shackles, was not part of the disciples' plan.

During Jesus' ministry, He taught repeatedly from the ancient Scriptures that the Messiah was, indeed, a king and divine eternal ruler who would restore peace in the world and end evil and suffering once and for all—but *not* in the same exact sense as the disciples believed. Jesus knew He was to first be a suffering servant. This fact escaped the disciples' attention at the time, but they came to understand it with dreadful clarity in the days that followed.

After Paul's conversion, he worded Jesus' purpose in a letter to a church in Philippi:

> *Make your own attitude that of Christ Jesus, who, existing in the form of God, did not consider equality with God as something to be used for his own advantage. Instead he emptied himself by assuming the form of a slave, taking on the likeness of men. And when he had come as a man in his external form, he humbled himself by becoming obedient to the point of death—even to death on a cross.* (Philippians 2:5-8)

That death, crucifixion, was an especially horrifying way to die. The shape of a cross is essentially the natural shape of a person standing with their arms extended sideways. Victims of crucifixion hung from their outstretched arms, which were nailed into the cross beam by the palms or wrists. Jesus' hands were pierced in this manner; however, the nails may not have held His entire weight nor been the cause of His death. They were simply part of the torture. Instead, it was the hanging aspect of crucifixion that brought death. With the full weight of the victims pulling down on their outstretched arms, their lungs compressed and filled with fluid, which, slowly but surely, led to asphyxiation.

To prevent a quick death, the Roman practice of crucifixion included a way for victims to stand or push up with their legs, which were nailed through the ankle or heel bones to the cross, periodically decompressing the lungs. Depending on the victims' survival instinct, this could prolong death for days. Yet, death was inevitable, from the sheer exhaustion of the effort as well as dehydration and blood loss, eventually resulting in complete muscle failure.

This was the manner in which Jesus was crucified. Because Jesus was executed on a Friday with the Jewish Passover about to begin, the Roman soldiers were urged to make sure Jesus was dead in time for burial before the celebration began. It was not uncommon to break the legs of the crucified to hasten their death, but the soldiers considered Jesus to be already deceased.[148] Instead, a soldier pierced Jesus' side and blood mixed with water, known today as pericardial fluid, came forth.[149] This is a sure indication of death.[150]

Some critics claim that the events following Jesus' conviction and torture never resulted in His final execution; that, although He suffered, He never died. Yet, the eyewitness testimony in the New Testament gospels of the crucifixion clearly shows Jesus had died.

Fact 2: Honorable burial

The gospels of Matthew, Mark, and Luke relate that Jesus was buried in the tomb of a member of the court of the Sanhedrin named Joseph of Arimathea. This means the location of Jesus' body would have been known by anyone suspicious of the claims of Jesus being alive. All they would have had to do is go and visit the tomb.

The manner in which the body of Jesus was handled after His death was done according to Jewish law. According to first century independent historical sources external to the New Testament, it was a Roman practice, although rare, to allow the bodies of crucified Jews to be given to their Jewish families from other Roman-occupied provinces for a proper burial.[151] Since the crucifixion was carried out in Jerusalem and the Passover was nigh, the order of the Jewish high council given to its member, Joseph of Arimathea, to have the body of Jesus properly buried makes complete sense. Normally, criminals suffering Roman crucifixion were not buried at all. They were simply discarded in a mass grave and eaten by dogs.

Fact 3: An empty tomb

A central truth of the Christian faith is that Jesus rose from the dead. If there was no resurrection, the very foundation of Christianity is destroyed and its faith pitiful. One of the greatest escape artists of all time, Harry Houdini, spent a lot of his time debunking mediums and spiritualists. I've often wondered, had he been faced with the task of inventing a resurrection, could he have pulled it off?

Several factors need to be taken into consideration in order to appreciate the full ramifications of the empty tomb of Jesus.

First, there is little question that the tomb of Jesus was empty, a historical fact that even the earliest antagonists of Jesus' resurrection did not challenge.[152]

Second, the New Testament records that the female followers of Jesus were the first ones to find the tomb empty, a fact that would not have been included if it was merely invented content, because women held such a lowly status in first century Judaism.

Third, a large stone of approximately two tons was used to seal the tomb. It would have taken more than a dozen or so men to roll or insert a stone into or in front of a tomb, which was usually carved in solid rock and was about the size of a small elevator.[153]

In addition, a Roman Emperor's seal—a large clay stamp attached with ropes—was added to the stone and tomb. This would have been a great hindrance to grave robbers or the disciples if they wished to steal Christ's body. Keep in mind, too, that the disciples were already in fear for their lives and had renounced Jesus and fled. It is highly unlikely they would even have wanted to steal the body, much less attempt the feat, to create the illusion of something that was never, in their minds, supposed to take place.

Next, the burial tomb of Jesus was under Roman guard. Because Jesus predicted His own resurrection, the high priests requested the guard, the equivalent of a squad of soldiers.[154] Based on the New Testament narratives, these guards were charged with sealing the tomb and protecting it day and night. The only way the disciples or anyone else could've stolen Christ's body would be if the soldiers were paid off or simply neglected their task. This is unlikely since, according to Roman law, a soldier's punishment for disobedience was to be stripped naked, tied to his spear, and burned alive. When the empty tomb was discovered, it was in pristine condition with no sign of conflict, and there's no record of any soldier being punished.

Finally, Jewish burial tradition would have required Jesus' body be encased in a linen cloth. During this process, about a hundred or more pounds of various spices and gummy substances were layered in so that the cloth eventually dried and hardened, similar to a cast set for a broken bone. They would then add a separate cloth for the face. Yet, the New Testament narratives reveal that the cloths were found in the tomb, and we can only deduce, based on the timing and the practice of Jewish burial, that the main burial cloths would have appeared as a bodiless, caved in shell of syrupy linens. We know from the gospel narratives that the face cloth was found, neatly folded, nearby. These factors make it highly plausible to conclude that God raised Jesus from the dead. Even then, an empty tomb alone is not evidence enough to make resurrection the most reasonable conclusion.

Fact 4: Appearances after death

Upon hearing the reports from the other disciples that Jesus was alive, Thomas the disciple wouldn't believe it unless he could see for himself. "If I don't see the mark of the nails in his hands, put my finger into the mark of the nails, and put my hand into his side, I will never believe!" (John 20:25). It wasn't until eight days later, when Jesus materialized in a locked room, that Thomas was afforded his requirements for accepting Jesus' resurrection. Jesus said, "'Put your finger here and observe my hands. Reach out your hand and put it into my side. Don't be an unbeliever, but a believer.' Thomas responded to Him, 'My Lord and my God!' Jesus said, 'Because you have seen me, you have believed. Those who believe without seeing are blessed.'"

Jesus not only appeared to Thomas; many others saw Him alive, leading to the quickly circulated eyewitness reports that Jesus was raised from the dead. In all, hundreds of people saw Jesus alive over the course of about forty days. Even Bart Erhman, a self-proclaimed agnostic atheist known for his criticism of the Bible, confirmed the disciples' belief in the resurrection when he stated, "It is undisputable that some of the followers of Jesus came to think that he had been raised from the dead."[155]

As my investigation into this last piece of the puzzle ended, it was my conclusion that, with the certain death of Jesus, His honorable burial, His empty tomb, and His appearances to many eyewitnesses, God did, in fact, raise Jesus from the dead. Was this the end of my sacred quest? Had I left anything unexamined? Would my skeptical mind be satisfied with what I had learned?

Chapter 27

Pondering the Evidence

"Now just think a moment and answer the question, 'What shall I do with Jesus who is called Christ?'"
Dwight L. Moody

Let's take a moment and look back at my sacred quest; where it began, why I embarked on this journey, and what I learned along the way. You may remember I went forward to receive Christ as my personal Savior at age 16, but did not experience a personal relationship with Him, a life-changing moment, until that fateful encounter on Interstate 10 three years later. My desire to connect with God moved me to make big changes in my life, but had I lost my skeptical logic in the process?

You may also remember that, one year later, at age 20, I decided that it was all too important to be intellectually confident of my faith, as faith is only as good as the object or person you put your faith in. I asked myself, "If I am so skeptical about all things paranormal, how is it that my belief in Jesus is an exception?" Was my encounter that night on Interstate 10 just an emotional experience that filled a void? Was I simply being duped? I wondered if I had placed too much trust in the people I admired who shared their faith with me. A friend whose own faith had been dampened advised me not be too dogmatic about issues of faith, suggesting my faith was a product of my youth and that I would "get over it eventually." I had to know if that was true.

I set out on my sacred quest, then, to see if I could "unmask Jesus." As I said, I was determined to apply both my open-minded curiosity and well-oiled skepticism to an examination of the person of Jesus Christ as well as the Christian faith. I was committed to an honest analysis that included looking at worldviews, paranormal claims, and tenets of the world's major religions that were in conflict with the Christian faith or to Jesus as the Messiah. I wanted to use the utmost discernment to divine the truth and recognize deception. I needed to be willing to closely examine and be completely honest with myself, "unmasking the masquerade" of my own personal superstitions and faith.

The End of the Journey

In my original quest, I sought an objective look at the facts. As years have gone by, I have found that how a person approaches the evidence can often color his concluding views. For me, I first began my historical Jesus quest with the fairly certain belief that a transcendent, eternal, and personal God existed. Through study and everyday living, several lines of evidence affirmed that such a belief was intellectually warranted. When inquiring about claims of the supernatural, these evidences from nature reasonably permitted me to have a level of open mindedness that allowed facts to lead to whatever logical conclusions were most reasonable.

As I've read the works of historians and scientists with varying views on topics such as life after death, the existence of God, and the possibility of miracles, I have noticed a trend; one's *starting* presuppositions will dictate the direction that person allows the evidence to take them. If a person believes or is open to the possibility of the existence of God, that leaves open the *possibility* of the laws of physics to be broken by such a transcendent, immaterial, timeless intelligence. Yet, that doesn't mean that if we don't understand how something works in nature or have an unexplained phenomenon, we simply insert God to explain it. What I am suggesting is to be open to the evidence.

If skeptics *begin* with the conclusion that supernatural things can *never* happen, when this bias is confronted with evidence for the miraculous, they can't follow wherever that evidence leads. In the end, it's that person's biased worldview that hinders (or allows) what they are able and willing to believe.

When taking the more unbiased or open-minded approach, the authors of this book have found that most claims of the supernatural do lack evidence for being genuine. However, when that same scrutiny is applied to the claims for miracles in the historic Christian faith, the evidence for the existence of God in nature and the evidence for the life of Jesus in history, it reveals that the miraculous is not only possible—but has occurred! We are followers of the Messianic claims of Jesus because of the evidence that supports them.

Myth, Magician, or Messiah

Jesus is not a myth, as proven by the eyewitness accounts. Jesus is not a magician, because His miracles were simply not possible by natural means in the first century or through the use of illusionist techniques. That leaves one option. Jesus is the Messiah, the Savior of all humankind. He is *my* Messiah.

I am a Christian and have dedicated my life and my craft to communicating with others the fulfillment of having a living faith in Jesus Christ. I encourage you to consider the evidence and then ask yourself, "If Jesus or His disciples were simply lying and pulling off the greatest scam of the last two millennia, why did they all allow themselves to be killed as martyrs for their belief? Why would they even invent such a story if they were expecting a completely different, conquering King?" They gave their very lives for what they saw and experienced. Untold others have done the same since then—and still do today, worldwide.

I leave you to come to your own conclusions. I'd also encourage you to delve deeper by reading some of the books we've listed in the Recommended Reading addendum. Enjoy your quest!

Conclusion

Fear Unmasked

Rod Robison

"Then you will know the truth, and the truth will set you free."
Jesus Christ, John 8:32

This book's title carries a lofty goal of "unmasking the masquerade" of deception, fear, and the supernatural; however, deception lives at the root. And, as we've pointed out throughout the pages of this book, all of us can be deceived when we fail to look behind deception's mask. Even magicians highly trained in the art of deception can be fooled.

When I picked up the phone one evening just over ten years ago, one of the last people I expected to hear on the other end was my magician friend Scott Wolf. I had not spoken with him for quite some time. "Rod, I'm in trouble," I heard him say, his voice trembling.

It's very possible you've seen Scott before. A video of one of his magic routines gone horribly wrong went viral on YouTube and was seen by millions more on television.

I was in the audience a few years prior to his phone call when Scott set his entire head on fire—not on purpose. He deceived himself into assuming that playing with fire—even as a seasoned and highly trained fire-breathing magician who had performed the stunt countless times—would never result in severe burns over his entire face.

I'd seen him perform the stunt flawlessly many times before. I say "stunt" because there's a difference between a "stunt" and an "illusion"; if he had been performing an illusion, there would have been no real fire or any real danger. Scott's fire breathing act was dangerous and, yes, it was real fire. Holding a blazing torch in one hand and two others not yet set aflame, he would open his mouth, stick his tongue out, and touch it with the ignited torch. Then, with his tongue on fire, he would set the other two torches aflame. Repeatedly blowing out and reigniting the torches with his mouth, with no apparent harm, Scott duly petrified his audience. But, he was just getting warmed up, if you'll excuse the pun. In an explosive conclusion, Scott would chug a couple of ounces of lighter fluid, hold one of the flaming torches at arm's length, and blow a massive ball of fire the size of a couch into the air.

The night of the accident, Scott got a little careless, lighting up his face and head like a six foot candle. Frantically patting his face in a vain attempt to extinguish the flames, he ran off stage while the audience gasped in stunned horror.

I was the first to reach Scott offstage. I found him face down in the stage right wing, the fire now extinguished. His first words were, "I can't believe I did that."

He was rushed to a nearby hospital and, after several painful procedures over the next few weeks, made a full recovery.

In his younger days Scott had abused alcohol and drugs, another form of deception that landed him in jail for a short stint—just long enough to start his road toward sobriety and become a follower of Jesus Christ. A few years after becoming a Christian, Scott began touring with a Christian performance ministry. Although he'd been clean of alcohol and drugs for several years and was determined to keep it that way, the boredom of life on the road with little accountability led him to let his guard down; the deceptive thought, "*I can handle it*," gained a foothold in his resolve; soon, his old habits returned.

After being forced to leave the ministry, Scott moved to Alaska where his downward spiral accelerated, sucking him into a seemingly hopeless life of meth and cocaine addiction. It was at that point that he picked up the phone and called me.

"I need help," he pleaded. "I have to get straight." The sound of his voice told me he wasn't kidding.

He filled me in on the last few years and his descent into drug-fueled deception. For a second time he had played with fire, and for a second time he was burned badly. This time not only physically, but emotionally and spiritually.

I told Scott I would help him under one condition. "I'll see if I can pull together some plane fare from some of our magician buddies and fly you to Tucson where you can get some help and accountability. But you have to promise me one thing. When you get off that plane you're going straight to Teen Challenge treatment center and enter their program."

Scott quickly agreed. I called Teen Challenge and told them Scott couldn't afford their program but he desperately needed them. They agreed to accept him and, true to his word, Scott stepped off the plane and into a new life.

His years-long road to recovery was not without its stumbles, but today Scott is the Director of Teen Challenge Ministry Institute where he oversees interns at eleven campuses across the Northwest, and he graciously allowed me to share part of his journey with you. By God's grace and Scott's determination, a magician who himself was badly deceived now helps men find their way out of the darkness of deception by introducing them to the Way, the Truth, and the Life, Jesus Christ.

Throughout the pages of this book we've focused on psychic deception to help illustrate the nature of deception itself and our vulnerability to it. When I began writing this book and invited my friends Adrian, Toby, and André to contribute, I hoped that it could be more than merely an exposure of deception as it relates to apparent paranormal phenomena, as fascinating as that topic is. I wanted that kind of deception to act as a poignant metaphor for whatever deception you and I struggle with daily. It's tempting to view people who are trapped in various types of psychic deceit as naïve and caught up in something we could never fall for. But the type of deceit we fall for isn't really the point. The real point that I hope you take with you is that we *do* fall for it. . . every day. Being aware of our own propensity to lose our footing when deceit crosses our path makes us much more aware of it when it does, inevitably and repeatedly, cross our path.

The Bible makes it clear that there is an enemy of our souls whose malevolent passion is to not only deceive us but, in the process, to destroy us. Here's how one of Jesus' closest followers, Peter, stated it: "Be alert and of sober mind. Your enemy the devil prowls around like a roaring lion looking for someone to devour" (I Peter 5:8).

That can be a terrifying realization and has, indeed, struck fear in the hearts of millions who have read those words over the centuries. Yet, as we've learned in our journey together, the Bible also tells us, rather paradoxically, that we are not to fear that roaring, deceiving enemy, "because, the one who is in you is greater than the one who is in the world [the spirit of the anti-Christ.]" (I John 4:4).

It's been said that the phrase "fear not" appears in the Bible 365 times—one for each day of the year. But that's not entirely accurate. While that phrase and "be not afraid" appear 103 times in the King James Version, there are hundreds more that tell us to fear God alone, do not be anxious, and do not worry.[156] Regardless of the phrase count, it's abundantly clear that we don't need to fear Satan when Christ is the King of our lives.

Beyond the assurances from Scripture that we need not be afraid, there is ample description of our enemy in the sacred pages to lead us to the conclusion that his stock-in-trade is deception and fear. Not God-like powers—which is merely a mask behind which he often hides—but deception and fear. Not conferring miraculous powers to humans as popular lore would have us believe.

Deception.

Fear.

Ultimately, our liberation from deception and fear is not dependent upon what our enemy can or cannot do. It is anchored firmly on what our sovereign God, the Creator of the universe, alone *can* and *does* do. He provided us all a Way out of that deception and fear through the Truth and Light–His Son.

It is our hope and prayer that, whether you know—as Jesus called Himself—*the* Way, *the* Truth, and *the* Life or are merely one seeking a way forward toward truth and light, that you'll continue on that path, because—as the New Testament book of Hebrews says in Chapter 11: "anyone who comes to him must believe that he exists and that he rewards those who earnestly seek him."

Anyone.

Recommended Reading

The Existence of God and the Historical Jesus

Habermas, Gary R. *The Historical Jesus: Ancient Evidence for the Life of Christ.* Joplin: College Press Pub., 1996.

Wallace, J. Warner. *Cold-case Christianity: A Homicide Detective Investigates the Claims of the Gospels.* Colorado Springs: David C. Cook, 2013.

Wallace, J. Warner. *God's Crime Scene: A Cold-case Detective Examines the Evidence for a Divinely Created Universe.* Colorado Springs: David C. Cook, 2015.

Defense of the Christian Faith

Bierle, Don. *Surprised by Faith.* 3rd ed. Greenwich: Global Publishing Services, 2012.

Craig, William Lane. *On Guard: Defending Your Faith with Reason and Precision.* Colorado Springs: David C. Cook, 2010.

Craig, William Lane. *Reasonable Faith: Christian Truth and Apologetics.* 3rd ed. Wheaton: Crossway Books, 2008.

Graham, Billy. *Just As I Am.* San Francisco: Harper Collins/ Zondervan, 1997.

Heeren, Fred. *Show Me God: What the Message from Space Is Telling Us About God.* Wheeling: Daystar Publications, 2000.

Lewis, C. S. *Miracles.* New York: Simon & Schuster, 1947.

Metaxas, Eric. *Miracles: What They Are, Why They Happen, and How They Can Change Your Life* New York: Penguin Random House, 2014.

Strobel, Lee. *The Case for Christ: A Journalist's Personal Investigation of the Evidence for Jesus.* San Francisco: Harper Collins/Zondervan, 2008.

Satan and Psychic Phenomena

Anderson, John. *Psychic Phenomena Unveiled.* Lafayette: Huntington House Publishers, 1991.

Arnold, Clinton. *Powers of Darkness: Principalities and Powers in Paul's Letters.* Downers Grove: InterVarsity Press, 1992.

Keene, M. Lamar *The Psychic Mafia,* Amherst: Prometheus Books, 1997.

Kole, André and Terry Holley, *Astrology and Psychic Phenomena,* Grand Rapids: Zondervan Publishing House, 1998.

Kole, André and Jerry MacGregor, *Mind Games,* Eugene: Harvest House Publishers, 1998.

Korem, Dan. *Powers: Testing the Psychic and Supernatural,* Downers Grove: Intervarsity Press, 1988.

Mulholland, John. *Beware Familiar Spirits: An Investigation into the Occult and Psychic Phenomena,* New York: Charles Scribner's Sons, 1938.

Simpson, Paul. *Second Thoughts,* Nashville: Thomas Nelson Publishers, 1996.

Wright, Nigel. *The Satan Syndrome,* Grand Rapids: Zondervan, 1990.

Historical Subjects

Brandon, Ruth. *The Spiritualists: The Passion for the Occult in the Nineteenth and Twentieth Centuries,* Knopf Publishers, 1983.

Bryan, Gerald B. *Psychic Dictatorship In America,* Livingston: Paolini International, 2000.

Hertenstein, Mike, an Jon Trott. *Selling Satan: The Evangelical Media and the Mike Warnke Scandal.* Chicago: Cornerstone Press, 1993.

Hill, Frances. *A Delusion of Satan: The Full Story of the Salem Witch Trials.* Old Saybrook: Tantor Publishing, 1995.

Houdini, Harry. *A Magician Among the Spirits,* New York, New York: Arno Press, 1972.

Oppenheim, Janet. *The Other World: Spiritualism and Psychical Research in England, 1850-1914*, New York: Cambridge University Press, 1985.

Polidoro, Massimo. *Final Séance: The Strange Friendship between Houdini and Conan Doyle,* Amherst: Prometheus, 2001.

Wicker, Christine. *Lily Dale: The Town that Talks to the Dead,* New York: Harper Collins, 2009.

THE EXPERTS WEIGH IN

Fellow illusionists, pastors, academics, expert contributors to the book and other students of these subjects weigh in on the controversial topics found in *Unmasking the Masquerade: Three Illusionsists Investigate Deception, Fear, and the Supernatural* or, "*Unmasking*" In addition, be sure to read André Kole's foreword for deep insights into the subject, page xiii:

"As I played an extremely small role in the construction of this book, I've been hesitant to recommend it for fear that the potential reader will see my opinion as biased. The fact is, I do recommend it for both Christian and secular audiences who are enraptured by false claims of the supernatural. As the book notes, there have certainly been events which are difficult, if not impossible, to understand, unless we know every detail involved in the situation; and even then, questions might remain. Unmasking the Masquerade addresses these challenges, and does so from a Believer's perspective, while keeping the facts squarely planted in reality."

Greg Edmonds—writer, illusionist, and student of magical history

"Since the earliest chapters of history, men and women in every culture have been hungry to encounter the God who created us all. But that same longing has often included a yearning for the paranormal – communicating with the dead, clairvoyance, and interacting with supernatural powers. Sadly, across the centuries there have been charlatans who, for a fee, have taken advantage of people's mystic fascinations through clever deceptions. The consequences for those taken in by these oily machinations has been immense. But the greatest tragedy has been their embrace of a counterfeit spirituality as a substitute for a relationship with our true Creator.

In 'Unmasking,' Rod Robison, Dr. Toby Travis, and Adrian Van Vactor pull back the curtain to reveal how these deceptions can occur. With humor, fascinating anecdotes, and lessons from history, the reader will come to better understand how we are all vulnerable to impostors and how to be more discerning about supernatural claims. And better yet, the reader will be pointed towards the one true God who loves us deeply. A page turner from start-to-finish, "Unmasking the Masquerade" is for every person who ever asked "How'd he do that...?"

Dr. Paul Simpson, forensic psychologist and author of *Second Thoughts*

"As a magician, a Christian, and a skeptic I fully stand behind what these three gentlemen have brought into the light. I have worked with Rod on several occasions as well as Adrian and Toby. I am also a former assistant and guest performer on the André Kole show, so I know firsthand the importance of what these men bring to the table and how important it is for the world to know how easy it is to be duped by someone using a simple magic trick to claim supernatural powers.

I love how Toby peels apart the fear section of 'Unmasking.' We look around us and people today are living in fear, 'the illudere' as Toby puts it. Toby makes it very clear in his section and quotes, 'As Christians, the Bible instructs us over and over again to fear God and God only. Apart from the fear of God, we are to live without fear for "greater is He that is in us than He that is in the world."'

We live in a world of lies, deceit, and distrust. However, the one thing that we can trust is the person of Jesus Christ and His Word. What these three men talk about is so vitally important as a guide to not get led astray. It only takes a magician to see the deception because they are very well trained in this area and I believe that God uses men like Rod, Toby, and Adrian to expose the lie and bring light to a darkened world."

Scott Wolf, Magician

"I have been a Magician for well over 35 years, and for the last 15, a Pastor. 'Unmasking' is a book that I wished I had had 15 years ago. Not only is it an excellent reference source for other publications dealing with fraud in the psychic realm, which is rampant and pervasive, but it provides some scriptural

support and insight into satan, his powers, and those of his minions. I gently disagree with Brother Rod's conclusion about satan's limitations, but he makes a solid layman's case for his position, which I greatly respect. I cannot recommend this publication high enough for both the lay audience, and the ministerial one; you will find no greater resource for dealing with the lies and deceptions of the 'psychic' scam business, and no finer effort at consolidating the information into one publication. I offer five stars for this, only because it won't let me give six!"

Pastor Timothy Walker BRE-pm/Bbl, MRE, MDiv-min

"'Unmasking' is a well written and researched book. I wholeheartedly recommend this book. It is a must read for all magicians and mentalists. I personally know two of the authors and can attest to their knowledge of the material discussed in the book and their expertise as performers."

LaMont McConnell, retired school psychologist and magician

"This is one of those rare books that I picked up and read through to the end in one day and even read parts of it again. I hope this book shows how easy it is to be fooled by TV shows and claims of supernatural powers that can so easily be done by trickery. Many people try to fill the hole in their heart with these things. But that hole can only be filled by the love of Jesus. This book should become a tool that will help turn people away from the lies of false prophets and to the saving truth of our Lord and Savior Jesus Christ.

'Unmasking' is both delightfully entertaining and determinedly educational. In this book, we are guided by three masterful illusionists—Rod Robison, Dr. Toby Travis and Adrian Van Vactor—who are determined to always emphasize the preeminence of reality over illusion. Furthermore, as the authors show through numerous case studies, while being deceived by well-meaning illusionists may be delightful, being deceived by ill-meaning charlatans may be disastrous. As Robison writes, 'it is important that we be aware of how deceptions are perpetrated so that we can discern truth' and thus evade 'the father of lies.' In this respect, as Travis duly emphasizes, 'In striking contrast to her neighbors ... we find a perpetual tendency in Israel to demythologize

life.' In short, in order to genuinely seek and find truth, we must be very careful not to confuse illusions with reality. On the flip side of deception, however, we must be equally careful not to confuse reality with illusions as well. Thus Adrian Van Vactor learnedly scrutinizes Jesus' miracles to ultimately conclude that Jesus Christ is not a myth nor a magician, but rather the promised Messiah of Israel. Indeed, to properly distinguish between reality and illusion is to discern truth properly; and to thus genuinely seek truth is to ultimately unmask the masquerade and find the God of truth."

Dr. Ron R. Rickards, physicist and author of *Eternal Harmony, Volume 1: The Unity of Truth in God*

"Unmasking' uses seasoned Christian illusionists, armed with the Scriptures, to expose deception in ways I never dreamed possible. I will surely recommend it highly for anyone with a curiosity for the paranormal, psychic or miraculous."

Kenneth E. Dewey, M. Ed.

"I am a seeker of truth; this book speaks volumes to anyone who sincerely desires to discover truth. 'Unmasking' is an important read in a day and time when culture buys into deception and fear as a norm. It is freeing and empowering. Rod Robison, Dr. Toby Travis and Adrian Van Vactor are vulnerable perhaps at their own expense but with a greater cause in mind: truth! If you truly seek truth you must read Unmasking the Masquerade."

Dr. Jeffrey Allen Love, pastor and author of *Life Palette: God Made a Masterpiece, and It's You!* and *Lord of the Fries: It's Not About Your Money, It's About Your Heart*

"'Unmasking' is like reading three books in one as it debunks what has captivated so many in search of a mystic experience. .. a great reference source… a theological treatise. . . a personal story. . . Fantastic!!"

Greg Walters, Broadcaster and Radio Station Manager

Notes

1 Interview with psychiatrist, Lynne D. Kitei, M.D., *The Phoenix Lights* (Charlottesville: Hampton Roads Publishing Company, Inc., 2004), 132-133

2 "Former Ariz. Governor Boosts UFO Claims," accessed December 6, 2016, http://www.nbcnews.com/id/17761943/ns/technology_and_science-space/t/former-ariz-governor-boosts-ufo-claims/

3 Leslie Kean, "Former Arizona Governor Now Admits Seeing UFO," accessed December 6, 2016, http://www.fifesymington.com/former-arizona-governor-now-admits-seeing-ufo/

4 André Kole and Terry Holley, *Astrology and Psychic Phenomena* (Grand Rapids: Zondervan Publishing House, 1998), 7.

5 Editor's note: The missionary Kole quoted was a few years off in his recollection of when the Billy Graham crusade occurred in Asunción. The event occurred about twenty years prior.

6 André Kole, personal communication, June 27, 2001.

7 Graham, Billy. *Just as I Am* (San Francisco: Harper Collins/Zondervan), 372-374.

8 M. Lamar Keene, *The Psychic Mafia* (Amherst: Promethius Books, 1997), 149.

9 Joe Nickell, "Paranormal Lincoln," accessed December 6, 2016, http://www.csicop.org/si/show/paranormal_lincoln.

10 *New York World*, October 21, 1888

11 *New York World*, October 21, 1888.

12 Wicker, Christine. *Lily Dale: The Town that Talks to the Dead* (New York: Harper Collins, 2009), 202.

13 Wicker, *Lily Dale,* 204.

14 *Arthur C. Clarke's World of Strange Powers,* "Fairies, Phantoms, and Fantastic Photographs," ITV, May 22, 1985, written by [screenplay/episode author].

15 Greg Edmonds, personal correspondence, October 29, 2016.

16 Harry Houdini, *A Magician Among the Spirits* (New York: Arno Press, 1972), 270.

17 http://www.christiananswers.net/q-eden/edn-r007

18 Joe Nickell, "John Edward: Spirit Huckster," accessed December 7, 2016, http://www.csicop.org/si/show/john_edward_spirit_huckster.

19 Jaime Franchi, "My Not-So-Psychic Experience with 'Long Island Medium' Theresa Caputo," accessed December 21, 2014, www.longislandpress.com.

20 Franchi, "My Not-So-Psychic Experience."

21 Linda Lyons, "One-Third of Americans Believe Dearly May Not Have Departed," accessed December 7, 2016, http://www.gallup.com/poll/17275/onethird-americansbelieve-dearly-may-not-have-departed.aspx.

22 Live Science Staff, "American's Belief in Paranormal Phenomena (Infographic)," accessed December 7, 2016, http://www.livescience.com/16748-americans-beliefs-paranormalinfographic.html.

23 Dan Korem, *Powers: Testing the Psychic and Supernatural* (Downers Grove: Intervarsity Press, 1988), 38.

24 Korem, *Powers*, 42.

25 Korem, *Powers*, 44-45.

26 Korem, *Powers*, 51.

27 Korem, *Powers*, 54-55.

28 Nina Bernstein, "On Welfare and Not Psychic? New York Provides Training," *New York Times,* January 28, 2000.

29 André Kole and Jerry MacGregor, *Mind Games.* (Eugene: Harvest House Publishers, 1998), 71-72.

30 Joe Turner, "Christian Magic: Theatrical Entertainment or Demonic Manifestation?," accessed December 12, 2016, www.christianpost.com

31 Korem, *Powers*, 91.

32 Terry Holley, personal communication, June 11, 2016.

33 André Kole and Terry Holley, *Astrology and Psychic Phenomena.* Grand Rapids: Zondervan, 1998), 18.

34 Kole and MacGregor, *Mind Games*, 18.

35 Kole and MacGregor, *Mind Games*, 166

36 Sir Arthur Conan Doyle, *The New Revelation* (London: George H. Doran Company, 1918), 23-24.

37. John Anderson, *Psychic Phenomena Unveiled* (Lafayette: Huntington House Publishers), 179.

38 Korem, *Powers*, 173.

39 Toby Travis, *Paranormal Lies and Wonders* (2009), 16.

40 Korem, *Powers*, 175.

41 Travis, *Paranormal Lies,* 16.

42 Reginald Scot, *The Discoverie of Witchcraft*, (London: William Brome, 1584). Accessed December 15, 2015, https://skullsinthestars.com/2009/09/22/the-discoverie-of-witchcraft-by-reginald-scot-1584/

43 Elaine G. Breslaw, *Witches of the Atlantic World: An Historical Reader and Primary Sourcebook* (New York: NYU Press, 2000), 504.

44 Author's note: In Chapter 13 we'll take a look at the fascinating psychological phenomenon of False Memory Syndrome.

45 Nigel Wright, *The Satan Syndrome* (Grand Rapids: Zondervan, 1990), 26.6

46 C. Peter Wagner and Douglas Pennoyer, Editors, *Wrestling with Dark Angels* , (Eugene: Wipf and Stock Publishers, 2001), 68- 69.

47 Murphy, *Wrestling*, 70.

48 C. Peter Wagner, *Wrestling with Dark Angels,* 306.

49 C. Peter Wagner, *Wrestling with Dark Angels,* 76.

50 André Kole, personal communication, June 27, 2001

51 Dr. Paul Simpson, *Second Thoughts* (Nashville: Thomas Nelson Publishers, 1996), 159.

52 Simpson, *Second Thoughts*, 159.

53 Simpson, *Second Thoughts*, 160.

54 Simpson, *Second Thoughts*, multiple cites.

55 Simpson, *Second Thoughts,* 46.

56 Simpson, *Second Thoughts,* 186-187

57 Simpson, *Second Thoughts*, 184.

58 Simpson, *Second Thoughts,* 187

59 Robert E. Bartholomew, Keith Basterfield, and George S. Howard, cited in Dr. Paul Simpson, *Second Thoughts* (Nashville: Thomas Nelson Publishers, 1996), 163.

60 S. C. Wilson and T. X. Barber, "The Fantasy-Prone Personality: Implications for Understanding Imagery, Hypnosis, and Parapsychological Phenomena." In

Imagery: Current Theory, Research and Application, ed. A. Sheikh (New York: Wiley & Sons, 1983), 340-390.

61 Simpson, *Second Thoughts.*

62 Jon Trott, "The Grade Five Syndrome," *Cornerstone*, 20, no. 96 (1991): 16

63 Simpson, *Second Thoughts*, 165.

64 Korem, *Powers*, 87-88.

65 Korem, *Powers*, 162.

66 Korem, Powers, 149.

67 Ellis, Blake and Melanie Hicken, "CNN Money Investigates: Maria Duval," accessed February 24, 2016, http://money.cnn.com/2016/02/24/news/maria-duval-victims/index.html.)

68 A video of one of the presentations of the Gospel used in these programs is available at https://www.youtube.com/watch?v=EVVHcK3Jgug&feature=youtu.be

69 Deuteronomy 6:13, 24; 10:12, 20; 31:12, 13; Joshua 4:24; 24:14; 1 Samuel 12:24 NASB

70 1 John 4:4 NASB

71 John 8:44 NASB

72 Clinton Arnold, *Powers of Darkness: Principalities and Powers in Paul's Letters* (Downers Grove: InterVarsity Press, 1992), 21.

73 JWM's Website, accessed October 25, 2016, http://www.jwm.christendom.co.uk.

74 John Warwick Montgomery, *Faith Founded on Fact* (Newburgh: Trinity Press, 1978), 180-181.

75 Mike Hertenstein & Jon Trott, *Selling Satan: The Tragic History of Mike Warnke,* Chicago: Cornerstone Press, 1972.

76 Erich Goode, "Two Paranormalisms or Two and a Half? An Empirical Exploration," *Skeptical Inquirer* 24:1 (2000).

77 For a greater discussion of this topic see: Dan Korem, *Powers: Testing the Psychic & Supernatural* (Downers Grove: Intervarsity Press, 1988), 54-55.

78 Robert L. Alden, *Theological Wordbook of the Old Testament*, ed. R. Laird Harris (Chicago: Moody Press, 1980), 572.

79 The full disclaimer can be found in Chapter 6.

80 Alden, *Theological Wordbook*, 17.

81 Merrill Unger and William White, *Nelson's Expository Dictionary of the Old Testament* (Nashville: Thomas Nelson Publishers, 1985), 242.

82 Dennis F. Kinlaw, "The Demythologization of the Demonic in the Old Testament," in *Demon Possession*, ed. John Warwick Montgomery (Minneapolis, MN: Bethany House Publishers, 1976), 33.

83 Robert T. Carroll, *The Skeptics Dictionary,* accessed December 12, 2016, http://skepdic.com/levitat.html.

http://skepdic.com/levitat.html.

84 John Anderson, *Psychic Phenomena Unveiled* (Lafayette: Huntington House Publishers), 182.

85 Anderson, *Psychic Phenomena*, 182.

86 Goldberg, *Theological Wordbook*, 90.

87 Jeane Dixon, *The Call to Glory* (New York: William Morrow & Company, 1971).

88 Norman Geisler, *Signs and Wonders* (Wheaton: Tyndale House, 1988), 28–30. Carl Murchison, ed., *The Case for and against Psychical Belief* (Worcester, MA: Clark University, 1927).

89 L. R. G. Crandon, "The Margery Mediumship: Experiments in Psychic Science," in Murchison, *The Case,* 104-105.

90 For more information on this topic see "Recommended Reading" at the end of the book.

91J oseph Jastrow, "The Animus of Psychical Research," in Murchison, *The Case,* 308.

92 Geisler, *Signs and Wonders,* 104-105.

93 John P. Newport, "Satan and Demons: A Theological Perspective" in Montgomery, *Demon Possession*, 326.

94 Newport, "Satan and Demons," in *Demon Possession*, 333.

95 R.F. Holland, "The Miraculous," A*merican Philosophical Quarterly 2*, no. 1 (1965): 49.

96 John Warwick Montgomery, *Faith Founded on Fact* (Newburgh: Trinity Press, 1978), 50.

97 Geisler, *Signs and Wonders,* 24.

98 C. S. Lewis, *Miracles* (New York: Simon & Schuster, 1947), 12.

99 Lewis, *Miracles*, 132.

100 Michiokakuvideos, "Michio Kaku on How Curiosity Is CRUSHED By The Education System," YouTube, accessed June 03, 2016. https:// www.youtube.com/watch?v=g32FQRyeu7M.

101 The "ideomotor effect" was previously defined in Chapter 5.

102 1 Corinthians 15:12-19, in *The Holy Bible: Updated New American Standard* (Anaheim: Foundation Publications, 2001).

103 Craig, William Lane, Reasonable Faith: Christian Truth and Apologetics (Wheaton: Crossway Books, 1994). See Part Two on the absurdity of life without God.

104 As a team member of the André Kole traveling program for several years, I became very familiar with the lines to the point where I could almost quote the entire show.

105 Bart D. Ehrman, *Did Jesus Exist?: The Historical Argument for Jesus of Nazareth* (New York: HarperOne, 2012), 12.

106 Ehrman, Bart D. Did Jesus Exist? *The Huffington Post.* Accessed June 06, 2016. http://www.huffingtonpost.com/bart-d-ehrman/did-jesus-exist_b_1349544.html.

107 F. L. Cross and Elizabeth A. Livingstone. *The Oxford Dictionary of the Christian Church*, 3rd ed. (Oxford: Oxford University Press, 2005), 908.

108 Flavius Josephus and William Whiston. *The Works of Josephus: Complete and Unabridged* (Peabody: Hendrickson Publishers, 1987), 18.3.3.

109 G. J. Goldberg, "The Coincidences of the Emmaus Narrative of Luke and the Testimonium of Josephus," Journal for the Study of the Pseudepigrapha 7, no. 13 (1995): 59-77, accessed December 12, 2016, doi:10.1177/095182079500001304.

110 Gary R. Habermas, *The Historical Jesus: Ancient Evidence for the Life of Christ* (Joplin: College Press Pub., 1996), 193.

111 Josephus and Whiston, *The Works of Josephus*, 20.9.1.

112 Habermas, *The Historical Jesus*, 193

113 Drcraigvideos, "Did Jesus Rise from the Dead? (William Lane Craig vs Richard Carrier)," YouTube, accessed June 08, 2016, https://www.youtube.com/watch?v=akd6qzFYzX8.

114 An early church creed would be an early oral tradition of the first followers of Jesus about what they witnessed.

115 "An Analysis of the Pre-Pauline Creed in 1 Corinthians 15:1-11," CARM: Christian Apologetics and Research Ministry, accessed October 28, 2016, https://carm.org/analysis-pre-pauline-creed-1-corinthians-151-11.

116 1 Corinthians 15:6

117 Ehrman, *Did Jesus Exist?*, 20, 96.

118 F. F. Bruce, *The New Testament Documents: Are They Reliable?* (Grand Rapids: Eerdmans, 1960), 123.

119 "The Jesus Seminar - Westar Institute," Westar Institute, accessed October 28, 2016, https://www.westarinstitute.org/projects/the-jesus-seminar.

120 Information about the Davinci Code: http://www.christianitytoday.com/history/2008/august/breaking-da-vinci-code.html

121 Habermas, *The Historical Jesus,* 55

122 Paleography is the dating of ancient manuscripts by the study of word usage, handwriting, language structures, and materials used to write on.

123 Carsten Peter Thiede and Matthew D'Ancona, *The Jesus Papyrus* (London: Weidenfeld & Nicolson, 1996).

124 "Did Copyists Copy the New Testament Correctly? - Daniel Wallace, PhD.," YouTube, accessed June 12, 2016, https://www.youtube.com/watch?v=AklwfTtAFoM.

125 Matthew 24:1-2; Mark 13:1-2; Luke 21:5-6 mention this prediction by Jesus. Note that John's gospel does not include the prediction and is considered the latest to be written, perhaps even after the destruction of the temple. It is, therefore, reasonable to see why John did not mention the temple as it was not relevant to his account.

126 Richard Bauckham, *The Testimony of the Beloved Disciple: Narrative, History, and Theology in the Gospel of John* (Grand Rapids: Baker Academic, 2007).

127 J. Warner Wallace, *Cold-case Christianity: A Homicide Detective Investigates the Claims of the Gospels* (Colorado City: David C. Cook, 2013).

128 "Dr. Daniel Wallace - How Badly Did the Scribes Corrupt the New Testament Text?" YouTube, accessed June 11, 2016, http://www.youtube.com/channel/UCTzSjZc3Pg0bDG5KIdrgwHQ.

129 Dr. Daniel Wallace. [Dr. Wallace is is a professor of New Testament Studies at Dallas Theological Seminary and 2016 president of the Evangelical Theological Society. In 2002, Wallace founded The Center for the Study of New Testament Manuscripts. During its brief history, CSNTM has collaborated with more than 40 institutions on 4 continents to produce more than 350,000 images of New Testament manuscripts. In the process, the Center has discovered more

than 90 New Testament manuscripts, many of which are viewable at their website.

130 Bruce, *The New Testament Documents.*

131 Habermas, *The Historical Jesus.*

132 Habermas, *The Historical Jesus.*

133 It's important to keep in mind that the very first followers of Jesus received intense persecution and death for believing and spreading Jesus' message. It is highly improbable they would have done so knowing Jesus was employing trickery to accomplish his miracles. Someone may die for something they *believe* is true but which isn't, but people rarely give their lives for something they *know* isn't true.

134 "Was Jesus the First Magician?" YouTube, accessed June 18, 2016, https://www.youtube.com/watch?v=RZY4bR_oJHA.

135 Mindreader, "Dynamo - Walking on Water and Arrested," YouTube, accessed June 18, 2016, https://www.youtube.com/watch?v=PeJveOOAgzA.

136 MrSpliterr, "Dynamo Walk on Water FAIL," YouTube, accessed June 18, 2016, https://www.youtube.com/watch?v=2Yx2hU9uv40.

137 Dictionary.com Unabridged, "functional disease," accessed: July 21, 2016, http://www.dictionary.com/browse/functional-disease.

138 Dictionary.com Unabridged, "organic disease," accessed: July 21, 2016, http://www.dictionary.com/browse/functional-disease.

139 "Placebo Effect," MedicineNet, accessed July 21, 2016, http://www.medicinenet.com/script/main/art.asp?articlekey=31481.

140 "Psychosomatic Disorders. Mind and Body Disorders," Patient, accessed July 21, 2016, http://patient.info/health/psychosomaticdisorders.

141 John 8:23

142 Mark 6:14-20, Luke 3:18-20

143 William Lane Craig, *Reasonable Faith: Christian Truth and Apologetics, 3rd ed.* (Wheaton: Crossway Books, 2008). 315-316

144 *Holy Bible: Holman Christian Standard Bible* (Nashville: Holman Bible Publishers, 2003).

145 John 19:19

146 Luke 18:31-34

147 Mark 8:31-38

148 John 19:32-33

149 John 19:34; Luke

150 William D. Edwards, Wesley J. Gabel, and Floyd E. Hosmer, "On the Physical Death of Jesus Christ," *Journal of American Medical Association*, 256 (1986):1455-1463.

151 Michael F. Bird, Craig A. Evens, Simon J. Gathercole, Charles E. Hill, and Chris Tilling, *How God Became Jesus: The Real Origins of Belief in Jesus' Divine Nature--a Response to Bart Ehrman*, Grand Rapids:: Zondervan, 2014, Kindle Edition, 75.

152 John Ankerberg, "4 Historical Facts That Prove Jesus Really Did Rise from the Dead," YouTube, accessed June 17, 2016, https://www.youtube.com/watch?v=RmKg62GDqF4. For a deeper explanation, see this interview.

153 "How Was Jesus' Tomb Sealed? - Biblical Archaeology Society," Biblical Archaeology Society, accessed August 04, 2016, http://www.biblicalarchaeology.org/daily/biblical-sites-places/jerusalem/how-was-jesustomb-sealed.

154 John 2:18-22; Matthew 12:39-40, 16:21, 27:62-64; John 10:17-18.

155 Ehrman, *Did Jesus Exist?* 183.

156 http://www1.cbn.com/soultransformation/archive/2011/10/21/fear-not.-365-days-a-year.

157 Springfield Union article, January 27, 1925: Houdini stirred by article may sue Sir Arthur. 1925. Image. Retrieved from the Library of Congress, https://www.loc.gov/item/varshoud.hs041/. (Accessed December 23, 2016.

158 "The Conversion of St. Paul" by Peter Paul Rubens (1577–1640), housed in the Courtauld Gallery, London. Photo used by permission, www.peterpaulrubens.org under the Creative Commons license, trimmed and converted to greyscale for print.

159 "Christ in front of Pilate" by Mihály Munkácsy (1844-1900), cropped and converted to greyscale for print, Public Domain, https://commons.wikimedia.org/w/index.php?curid=230979.

Unmasking the Masquerade

www.unmaskingthemasquerade.com

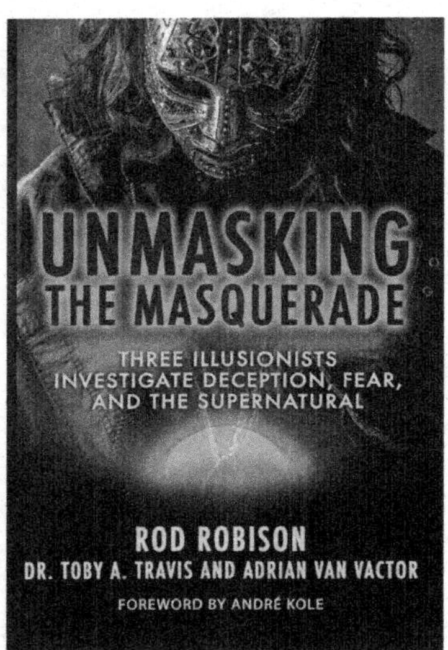

Connect with the authors to arrange interviews, speaking engagements, special events and book signings or see upcoming events.

Connect with the publisher for special bulk pricing.

Find links to online resources and information about other formats of this title, available online and through your favorite bookstore.

Have a question or comment?

Find us and post on Social Media!

Do you have an opinion about this book?
Your opinion is valuable to us.
Please post your review and comments on Amazon.

CPSIA information can be obtained
at www.ICGtesting.com
Printed in the USA
FSOW03n1619110117
29332FS

9 780996 206792